I , 95

Mid-Atlantic

by

A. Bowditch

"On the I, do I things, think I thoughts."

AB

I, 95

Dedicated to my family who had to wait for me all over the East Coast while I was dreaming...

Lilian, David, Bridget, Jennifer...

and Mom.

Table of Contents

PROLOGUE	7
BOWDITCH'S LAWS OF THE I	9
INTRODUCTION	11
SPACE, THE FIRST FRONTIER	15
DRIVEAGE	33
I GAMES	53
JAMS	57
I POLICE	61
SIGNAGE	67
ETIQUETTE AND DISETIQUETTE	75
DUTY BOOTHS	83
TRUCKIN'	87
LANEAGE	91
I NICETIES	95
FOODAGE	101
PLACE NAMES	113
MAPPAGE	117
ODDITIES	123
1610 AM	129
CONSTRUCTION	131
EXERCISE	135
GLOSSARY	139
QUIZ ANSWERS	153

I, 95

PROLOGUE

The Interstate Highway system was conceived by the Department of Defense during the Eisenhower administration as a way to perform massive troop movements quickly. It was originally called *The National System of Interstate and Defense Highways*. Every overpass had to have a sixteen foot clearance to allow a missile on a truck to pass safely underneath. Talk about your moving targets! But, be that as it may, eventually *you*, though possibly not as an employee of the Department of Defense nor having a large ICBM behind you on that vacation trailer, will end up on the Interstate Highway System... the I.

This book was conceived and verbalized while traveling on this amazing example of modern engineering, specifically the corridor between Fredericksburg, Virginia and Saddle Brook, New Jersey, with side trips to friends in other locations[1]. It was written because of the observed driving habits and idiosyncrasies of many of the other travelers (coroaders) on the I with me at the time. We all had a common objective, to get to our destinations in one piece, but we all had different means to our ends. This book is just a dissertation on those differing means and habits. Future plans are to travel other portions of the I in other portions of the country and report on those.

---

[1] And I will now acknowledge their warm friendship and hospitality. Thanks everyone.

Throughout this publication there are new terms introduced to define objects, actions, and concepts. These are not here to confuse the reader[2], they are introduced to synchronize the reader to a new lingo associated with something we have all been doing for years, but never knew the language, except to us old CB'ers. But even this language has changed. To this end, I have included at the end of this document a glossary to allow both neophytes and experts alike the opportunity to interpret the seeming gibberish included here. It is recommended that the reader read or peruse the glossary first, if only to become familiar with the terms and coinages used. Believe me, this will help.

For the reader's entertainment and curiosity, there are scattered throughout the book[3] questions to make you stop and think, or stop and laugh. These questions are answered at the end of the book.

QUESTION: Why is it called a "glossary?"

---

[2] Well, maybe a little.
[3] Actually, there is no scattering at all. They are very well organized and appear only at the end of each chapter.

BOWDITCH'S LAWS OF THE I

FIRST

The less time you have to get to a destination, the more likely you will encounter traffic.

SECOND

Important signage will be displayed improminantly or out of sight.

THIRD

Anything that flashes has to be important. The importance of flashing signage will be directly proportional to the number of lights which are burned out.

I, 95

FOURTH

The Left Lane is not the fastest.

FIFTH

The lane you are in at the duty booth is the slowest.

SIXTH

Rocks dislodged from trailers carrying earth moving equipment act in perfect harmony with the chaos theory.

INTRODUCTION

We all travel by auto at some point in our lives. For almost all of us, our first trip is within days of being introduced into this world. It starts at birth. We get out of the hospital and we get into a car. Then we get on the Interstate: The I. According to the American Automobile Association there were 175,128,000 licensed drivers (autotators) in the United States in 1994. Many of them are out there on the I the same time you are. Sometimes it seems that they are *all* out there. It is rumored that there is not enough room on New Jersey roads for all the automobiles registered there. And many of those that did fit would be in potholes.

To become as pleasurable as possible, driving on the I has to be perceived as an art form. It has to be defined not only by the rules of the road, but by the legitimate, courteous methods one uses to get from that proverbial Point A to Point B in the same proverb. Driveage has to be enjoyed, a thing of beauty and a work of art. It must become not the ends, but the means. To reach those means we have to cooperate with an *awful* lot of people.

Long Distance Traveling is in the rear of the beholder. The autotator has to sit for the entire trip[4]. To some people, going to the mall is a long distance, while to others, five hours is around the block. To quote some long forgotten advertisement "It's not how long you make it, it's how you make it long." Even a short trip can seem like an eternity if not performed properly and with

---

[4] There is only a small amount of limited exercise the autotator can perform, a subject approached in the EXERCISE chapter.

I, 95

some amount of planning. Nevertheless, driving, whether on the I or on your local low-speed roads, can be enjoyable and should be practiced so as to refine the art form that it is. With that practice, it can be mastered and thus can be applied with all diligence and grace necessary. But it does require patience and work. Autotators today tend to take any kind of driving for granted, be it short or long distance. We have memorized many of the rules of the road to the point that they are second nature[5]. We don't have to think about which side of the road to be on or what the octagonal red sign means. So let's go back and think about driving, especially on the I, where speed is king and time flies by as quickly as the skip lines.

    I have been driving for 32 years. I have received one ticket for a moving violation[6], but I have never been involved in or caused an accident. I am bragging, and I am proud of my accomplishment. Some people take pride in the number of violations they have received and have wallpapered their garage with the lovely little pieces of paper. That is fine, but at what cost? I have not room, money, nor time to wallpaper; I spend so much time in my vehicles. Yes, there are many people who drive more on the I than I do, but not very many with my record. Unfortunately, it seems that there are too many people out there with stories about being involved in some sort of fender bender: the secretary arrives at work late and immediately calls her insurance agent; the bent, dented 1970 Toyota seen in every state except Alaska; they all have stories.

    The secret to my success is nothing more than using attention on the details of driving. Traffic patterns, flotsam and jetsam, coroaders, and the ever-present UMCs all have to do

---

    [5] With the exception of the Virginia law that states that you must have your headlights on if your windshield wipers are on.

    [6] Of course, there were mitigating circumstances.

with my getting to my various destinations successfully. When I am in steerage, I am driving. If I wanted to see sights, I would take a bus or a train or, heaven forbid, have someone else drive. But I want to drive because I am good at it and I enjoy doing it, as everyone who wants to own a driver's license should[7]. Driving is an art form, and as such, can be improved and refined. Many people make it a task, but if you have to make that long trip to Grandma's or to that faraway job site, you might as well make it enjoyable and improve your skills. Define that art form so others may enjoy it. And that driveage requires responsibility.

Let's face it, from the day you get your learner's permit you are smitten. It is a fact that on the first day you get your permanent license, you put more miles on Mom and Dad's family wagon than any other day in your life. After that, Mom and Dad's family wagon is a disgrace to be seen driving. That means get a job, get a car, and get a can of car polish. And the car polish is just the start. After that there's the fabric cleaner, the plastic cleaner/restorer, the touch-up paint, the rubber cleaner, and the detailer polish. Plus the Autorags, the old T-shirts necessary to apply all of the aforementioned items[8]. Trips to the Laundromat include whites, darks, and autorags. The neater the auto, the neater you feel. Much has been written about the "love affair" that automobile owners in the US of A have with their chariots; that love affair is not going to be rehashed here. But the affair blossoms because the automobile is an individual statement, it is our "space" to customize the way we

---

[7] You do not really own your driver's license. It can be taken away by the proper authorities. In Virginia, up to the age of 18, the "proper authorities" can be your parents, for any reason.

[8] T-shirts are only mentioned here as a catch-all item. Autorags actually vary from the old pair of white socks to the incredibly expensive chamois for getting the water off of the incredibly clean paint job.

I, 95

desire and not have to answer to anyone[9]. It is the Calder mobile that we have near total control over, with only few things that the government makes us do, like lights and brakes and directionals and seat belts. Again, responsibilities.

Now we are ready to move that art form down the highway so that you and everyone else can enjoy it, and do it safely. There is only one way to protect your work of art and that is to drive defensively. Defensive driving is the only way to drive. Protect yourself and your investments.

The reward for concentration and defensive driving, having been totally, functionally integrated with the rest of the coroaders, is the satisfaction of having traversed life's major highways commingled with coroaders and, with each one, safely reached respective destinations. This is Point B-ing. It is the sensation you get when you pull into the driveway of your destination safely, completely. True Point B-ing? But that's the end of the I. First we have to prepare.

QUESTION: If every licensed driver in the United States were on the I at the same time, how many automobiles per mile would be there?

---

[9] Within limits. Some states have regulations on window tinting, dangling objects attached to the interior rirmir, or lighting options. In Virginia, you can have no blue lights on your vehicle. Bluelights make your vehicle look too much like a police car. I am sure there is a good reason for that.

SPACE, THE FIRST FRONTIER

"Creature comfort, above all else. I am the creature"

AB

In their car, everyone creates their own world, their own spaceship transversing the cosmos of the I. That world is the Space between the windows that autotators will guard with their lives and their Clubs[10]. The autotator defines the Space, creates a world within which he or she is the royalty, the king or queen, the prince or princess. It is this world which they move down the road, motivated by destination, energized by gasoline, and limited only by duty booths, traffic lights, and the occasional Jam.

Creation of the Space takes much consideration. The comfort of the throne, the position of the steerage, the location of the liquid refreshment... all of these and more require careful thought and attention to detail. Each time we elect a new president, the First Lady redefines the contents of the White House primarily to spend as much of the taxpayer's money as possible, and secondarily to make things more comfortable[11]. We do the same with our automobiles, only we don't affect the National or Local Debt quite so seriously.

---

[10] The Club™ is an interesting name for this security device. It implies prehistoric man defending his cave. I have always wondered if Fred and Barney had any problems with car thieves.

[11] Ever wonder what happens to the "old" stuff? US of A's First Lady's Yard Sale. Once every four years, some time around the end of January.

I, 95

Everyone's Space will be different. That's one of the things that make us unique. The following list contains items determined as Some of the Items to Consider as Most Important in the Creation of the Space. It is by no means a comprehensive list, but it contains those items that should be considered when planning purchasing or modifying a vehicle which will be transporting you on voyages down the I.

THRONES

First and foremost, the throne must be comfortable. You're going to be sitting there a long time, it may as well be cozy, and this means it has to be adjustable. It has to be adjustable enough so that not only you, but also your teenage daughter can be comfortable, too. You have to realize that at some point in the life of your automobile, your teenage prodigy will drive it.

Cows are nice to look at and touch, but sit on one of those puppies when the car has been sitting in the mall parking lot for a few hours in the summer and it's "Oh Mama!" until the air (if so equipped) kicks the cow down to a cooler level. Use of a crashboard screen with some cute slogan or pair of eyes is a must to keep the sun out of the inside. It's worse in the winter. You're afraid that the cow will crack under the pressure, and it will take a long time for your body heat to bring it back to tolerable. Carry a back pocket bun warmer if you insist on cows. Electric socks are an incredible invention, but I don't think electric underwear is quite yet a marketable item[12]. Cows also take a lot of maintenance. And no one covers them. You got a

---

[12] Although it is available for motorcyclists.

cow, you might as well show it off. Nothing tackier than nice cows with flannel overwear or clear plastic trim.

Velour or cloth thrones are the most comfortable for going I distances. This upholstery allows a certain amount of air flow around your contact points[13], and the throne won't play the heated cow in the summer. In the winter, velour and cloth do not retain the coolth as well, so when you sit down, they seem to pick up your body heat rapidly. If taken care of properly, they can last. If you drink soda, try Sodaguard[14]. My truck has tacky flannel overwear, but only to cover the tackier plastic seats. The overwear has pockets all over it, great for maps, loose change, flashlights, and other typical roader necessities. Covering your throne with an old towel, no matter what picture or cute saying is imprinted on it, is incredibly tacky. People now are installing those bead blankets which are supposed to increase the body's circulation of important fluids and feel comfortable. Just wait until one of the ridiculously flimsy light-weight fishing lines lets go. You'll be picking wooden balls out of the upholstery for weeks.

An electrically adjustable throne is really the item, especially if it has memory. Infinitely adjustable, you can set that throne to your body shape and it's a touch of the button to bring the memory of your posterior back into reality. And it won't moan or groan or make snide comments. But all those little electric motors are just more items to break down. One car company even has an advertisement that extols just the motors under the seat. With gold contacts. That's tacky. Sell the car to a dentist when it's about to go. "My tooth filling was found under the

---

[13] Nicely put, huh?
[14] Scotchguard™ works too, but drinking scotch and driving should not be in anyone's book.

I, 95

front seat of an Audi!" The scandal sheets could have a field day with a story like this.

If so equipped, put the headrest all the way up, as far up as you can get it. The typical headrest is typically small, so it will not block your vision, but in the down position they will serve only to be uncomfortable if you are butted. If you put the headrest up as far as possible, you can slam your head back, stretch your arms out straight and not lose your perspective. Some automobile manufacturers have installed seats with permanent, non-adjustable headrests. Before buying an automobile with these, test drive it on the I for a few miles and make sure it is for you.

Electrically heated seats are now available on many vehicles. Oh, the joy of a warm throne on a cold winter's morn! But, if you have enough money to afford an electrically heated throne, someone else must be doing the driving. Now we need heated copilot seats. But... we do not want to make copilots too comfortable. They need to stay awake too.

One side note here ... For some physical reason, women tend to sit closer to the steerage unit than men. Ladies, this could be dangerous. For one thing, stretching your arms out straight is good for all kinds of circulation. For two things, sitting too close to the baggy can be hazardous to your health. In a frontal bender, the baggy literally explodes from the steerage unit at some incredible mileage per hour, forcing you back into the seat rather rapidly. Sitting too close to it will cause you to be punched in the face rather fiercely. Sit back, stretch your arms and legs, relax.

One argument against straight-arm driveage is that the backbone is not straight in this position. Adjust the throne position, then. There is an answer. But keep away from the baggy.

STEERAGE UNITS

The typical steerage unit is nothing to write home about. A ring of plastic used to direct your steed. If you have a unit with no covering, just plain plastic, I recommend getting one of those leather covering kits. It will look good, feel good, require only a little maintenance, and the grip is almost perfection, much better than cold plastic. Just remember when you install it to lace it up as tight as it will go, then after a few weeks, re-lace it, as it will stretch somewhat. Nothing like taking a high speed turn and having the steerage unit slip out of your grip. Guaranteed to challenge the most agile. Not unlike making love in a canoe with a loose condom, standing up.

Make sure the steerage unit is thick or thin enough for your grip. Going from thick to thin in a day is awkward. Changing your grip to handle the thin plastic after handling a thick cow cover for a few hours is not easy. Also the position of the spokes is important. Most every new automobile is equipped with a baggy now, which will cause thick and widely spaced spokes, but make sure you are comfortable with the relative height of the spokes and the finger-width between them. It's important to change your grip every now and then if for no other reason than to keep the body fluids circulating. If there is no room between the spokes for the phalanges, the number of finger positions will be limited and, thus, uncomfortable.

If your steerage unit has tilt, change the position every so often just to remind you where you are. You can learn new grips when that puppy is all the way up or all the way down. Just make sure that when it is in the "normal" position the important part of the gauges are visible. As autotator, you should be able to see the prime parts of the speedo and the tacho, and the oil pressure, ammeter, and water temperature gauges[15]. Gauges are important. As prime autotator, if you do not know how to read the gauges, you should learn. They provide Triple I[16].

LIQUID CONTAINMENT UNIT (LCU)

A comfortable mug for coffee or iced drinks is very important. I trips require liquid refreshment. The Styrofoam units from the Roy's[17] for containment of said liquids are absurd. One white-knucklin', cut 'em off grip in a jam and there's liquid all over something, more than likely, you. A good LCU has two holes in the top so you do not create a vacuum while sipping, a phenomenon known as "sip-sucking." Nothing worse than pulling into a duty booth with your LCU stuck to your face. The area of the LCU you plan to sip from should be recessed. This allows a slight amount of cooling of the liquid, if necessary[18]. That terrible burning sensation on the lips at 70 miles per hour is hard to nurse. Find an LCU which meets the following criteria:

Has a good handle - A handle is an absolute necessity. Do not rely on an LCU without one. Handleless LCUs cannot be trusted, they will turn on you. The handle serves to point the sipping hole in the right direction.

---

[15] Idiot lights are all right as long as you know how to react to them. That should be to pull over, stop, and turn off the engine.

[16] Incredibly Important Information.

[17] Roy Roger's or other appropriate fooder.

[18] This is the "cooling pool." Of course, if the liquid is already cool, the slight recess in the top of the mug will be used to slightly warm the liquid; a boon for people with cold-sensitive teeth.

Has a lid on it which snaps tight - The harder it is to remove the better. When (not *if*) you drop it, you do not want to have to stop and clean up the mess.

Is the right color for the interior - A carefully selected LCU will not clash with the interior of the vehicle, it will serve to enhance it and display your good taste.

Doesn't say anything on it which could remotely offend truck drivers, motorcycle gangs or other major sections of the populace - No sense taking any chances of having a carefully selected LCU destroyed by indiscretion.

Fits properly into the LCUL (see next) - A poorly fitting LCU will only tip over.

"Thermal" mugs are an amazing invention. They have the ability to keep hot liquids hot and cold liquids cold. It is amazing that they can discern the difference and remember which is which.

A Harley-Davidson travel mug is highly recommended. If you have one of these, everyone will think your other car is a Harley and show you incredible respect. And black goes with everything.

LIQUID CONTAINMENT UNIT LOCATION (LCUL)

For long drives, the LCUL is very important. Reaching the LCU should require *no* exertion on your part. It should take no more effort than reaching for the AU controls. Of course, size of the LCU will determine its location, so plan well. If you are buying a new car, the LCUL should be number two or three on the list of purchasing considerations.

One of the great challenges of modern I driving is the LTT, or Liquid Transfer Task. Speeding along the I and running out of your favorite elixir can be traumatic. But you suddenly realize that you still have 12 drops of the requisite liquid in the original container from the Roy's[19]. So you simply perform a little patellage, rip the lid off of the old cup, rip the lid off of your favorite LCU, pour from the flimsy styro to the LCU, snap the lid back on the favorite, replace the lid on the empty styro, and toss the old deftly into the back seat or other appropriate TC. This maneuver actually requires three hands and a knee, but with a little practice, it can be performed easily. Simply start off by putting your favorite LCU between your legs. But one knee is in patellage. This means that you have to put the LCU right up there in your crotch. The liquid you are transferring may be 212 degrees Fahrenheit or 0 degrees centigrade[20]. The wrong bump at this time could be devastating, not to mention ruin your pants[21]. Careful selection of road location and road condition is a must for successful LTT. One optional LTT maneuver can be performed with the pinkie finger graciously wrapped around the steerage unit: Pinkage. Pinkage is not recommended in the mall

---

[19] Fooders being what they are, you can only purchase sizes of items which are far too small or far too large to fit into any LCU you use.

[20] One lady even sued a company because the coffee was too hot. No one knows exactly what she wanted when she ordered hot coffee. Soon the government will require labels on containers - "WARNING - THE LIQUID IN THIS CONTAINER IS ROOM TEMPERATURE!"

[21] For women who wear skirts while driving, don't, unless you absolutely have to. It is much more comfortable to wear loose slacks. If you really must wear a skirt and perform an LTT, practice pinkage because the crotch-based LTT is impossible, unless you are wearing a *really* short skirt and have thighs like bricks. If your thighs are like bricks, you shouldn't be wearing a skirt that short.

parking lot because it limits the LTT to four fingers, but then, we are not talking about driveage in the mall parking lot here. Never perform an LTT on a bridge or in a tunnel. Nighttime LTT is much more of a challenge. It requires considerable concentration and is sometimes called The LTT of the Dark Side. Proper and accurate LTT can be simplified greatly by a suitably thought out LCUL.

COPILOTS

Copilot is another term for the much older "shotgun," which dates back to the Stagecoach I. On the modern I, avoid them, copilots or shotguns. Unless you absolutely cannot perform any driving functions without human co-autotation, copilots only serve to annoy. They are, by nature and function, sight-seers, and all they want to do is to point out all the interesting things to you along the way, totally distracting you from your appointed driveage responsibilities. If they are not sight-seeing, they are finding fault with your driveage, certain grounds for divorce or ejection, totally justified. Make them read a book; *War and Peace* comes to mind, but definitely not *this* book. If they insist that they will get motion sickness when they read, make them walk. If you *must* have a copilot, create a lot of waste and give them the Sanitation Engineering functionality. If necessary, tasks such as Environment Control or Audio Unit Adjustor may also be assigned. If you think you need to talk to someone, the coroaders are there for your pleasure.

Coroaders are great listeners. They will never disagree with anything you tell them and will not blanch if you tend to use foul language; just make sure your windows are up and the heater or air conditioner is on full bore. Most of them even understand

I, 95

Sanskrit and many other foreign languages. Many of them are probably talking to you at the same time, in varying languages, carrying on a wonderful conversation with you without you even knowing about it. See how simple it is? You talk to them and they talk to you. And there are no interruptions in the conversation, because no one will disagree with anything you say. This is the only time during the trip that everyone agrees with everyone else. Just imagine what the consequences would be to world peace if everyone just got in their automobiles and drove the I. All those world leaders out there on the I with you, agreeing with everything you say.

Coroader group sing-a-longs are a lot of fun. They will remind you of sitting around the campfire toasting marshmallows. Only the campfire is doing 70 miles per hour. Just don't start "99 Bottles of Beer on the Wall." No one likes that song anymore.

If you cannot carry on a conversation with another human being, copilot or coautotator, use the copilot seat headrest. Just push the copilot seat all the way forward and it will seem like the copilot is sitting there. You can get pretty friendly with it. Put a wig or a hat on it, put your arm around it. Like coroaders, it will not talk back or vilify your driving skills. It will, if so desired, always smile and congratulate you on that last high-speed lane change. It will agree pleasantly with everything you do and say. Sort of like the perfect mate.

The last, although not completely recommended, copilot is the inflatable dummy, or Blowup. It is believed that this form of coautotator may talk back to you and has been known to criticize some driving responses. The blowup may also lead the autotator into a false sense of security in an HOV lane. If you are caught in the HOV lane during the illicit hours with a blowup, the police will frown on your companion. Blowups have been arrested for solicitation and taken away in a bubble. A deflating embarrassment. The mutual disrespect between blowups and the gendarmes dates back to the 19th century when horse riders used scarecrows as traveling companions in HOH[22] lanes. Many of the constabulary were insulted that the scarecrow got to ride a horse while the policeman was relegated to a bicycle.

AUTOPILOT

Known as "cruise control", this option is made more and more available on more and more models by more and more manufacturers. It will soon be more prevalent than a cigarette lighter[23]. No doubt about it, autopilot is a great option for the I. Set the gooser, hit the button, and stretch your right leg. But autopilot creates some special problems. Of course, it is impossible to use in near jam conditions. And to turn it off temporarily, the brakes need to be tapped. This shows the coroader behind you that you are going red, thus creating apprehension in them that you intend to stop. So they go red. The result is inevitable. But on a good, relatively empty stretch of the I, autopilot is great.

Recent Independent University[24] research has turned up an interesting autopilot fact: the electronic "black box" involved in creating this system actually has a brain of its own, totally separate from the vehicular "black box" which, when it breaks down, disables the entire vehicle. When you set the autopilot, all you are really doing is causing this system to maintain the needles on the speedometer and tachometer (if so equipped) at

---

[22] High Occupancy Horse.
[23] Cigarette lighters are almost obsolete. The receptacle is being replaced with a "power connector."
[24] A small coed University in Indiana.

the desired position. Another part of the system supplies the appropriate amount of fuel to the appropriate mechanisms to attempt to keep the automobile at the speed you requested. But sometimes these systems go to sleep[25] and you find yourself inexplicably slowing down or speeding up against your best wishes. Glancing at the speedometer or tachometer only proves that the needles are set at the same location you originally set them. When the systems wake up (after you are yelling profanities at the top of your lungs), they slowly adjust the speed to what it really should be. These systems feel no remorse.

AUDIO UNIT (AU)

This is probably the most important item in your automobile for driveage. A bad AU can ruin an I voyage. If you can't hear it, you can't sing to it.

The AU must have at least 50 Watts of power, not just for allowing the coroaders to hear your favorite music, but also to pull in that special station from Duluth while you are in New York. Four speakers are a must so that when you need all the windows down (about an hour after stopping at that last fooder, bless that burrito), you can switch to the front speakers when the wind noise drowns out the rears.

The choice of music is strictly personal. Many people would enjoy Beethoven or Bach for hours on end, while some others would enjoy listening to music wailed by Nine Inch Nails. The majority of autotators fall somewhere in between. The only criterion is that you don't force coroaders to enjoy your music with you, at least too much. That Taker at the duty booth has his

---

[25] As you may if you rely too heavily on autopilot.

or her own AU on, so respect them when dispersing coin of the realm. If you have gone for the top of the line AU and have a CD player built in, lucky you. Great quality music and a target for all the AU thieves in the world. Protect your investment. And treat those CDs well. If you are a taper[26], the music is completely customizable while you are homebound. This is a great way to go because you can put all your favorites on a few tapes or CDs and have one great sing-a-long on the way to Point B-ing. If you are stuck with just a radio, take a second job and buy a top of the line stereo (and security system) for the auto. You will not regret it. There are many long tunnels in the world, and very few of them have radio stations in them. And if you hit traffic in there, not only will you completely lose it to claustrophobia, but there will be nothing to listen to while you lose your mind.

For years now books have been available on cassette tapes. These books range from novels to "self-help" books designed to get you through the rigors of life. These cassette books are perfect for I journeys. If you are listening to this book right now, you are obviously caught up in some sort of time distortion which, if you rewind this tape right now, will take you back to the start of your journey. If you are near Point B-ing, DO NOT REWIND THIS TAPE!

Ancillary AU equipment is a drumstick. Take one along with you and beat out that rhythm on various items on the crashboard. Just beware of two things: you don't want to dent or break anything which may be of use later on, and you do not want to set off any baggies.

---

[26] Tape the music at home before the I voyage. Now it's easy to burn a CD for your listening enjoyment.

PORTABLE TAPE RECORDER

One of the greatest inventions for the dedicated roader is the personal, portable tape recorder. It uses those tiny, losable tapes which are dirt cheap. You're alone, zipping down the I and that most perfect thought strikes you, everything is so clear. But how do you record it? If you have one of those windshield notepads hanging by its suction cups on the inside of your windshield, you could grab the elusive pen or pencil and scribble the thought on the postage stamp sized piece of paper while driving underneath the semi[27] in front of you. But if you have the tape recorder, all you have to do is turn it on and create your perfect play-backable thoughts. Voice activated recorders are not recommended for driveage. Most any road noise will set them on and recording. Perfect thoughts, imperfect recordings. Don't forget to turn the AU down or off, and close the window. Otherwise, you will play it back later and find out that perfect thought is nothing but background noise. If you are in a convertible, you are in trouble, the background noise will be recorded as the thought unless you scream. Then coroaders will be only too aware of your innermost thoughts. The windshield post-its are a cute idea, but the effort to record the thought is better applied to the AU or steerage. Besides, while reaching for the memo pad, you may accidentally get the radar detector or the compass and then you'll be pulled over for having your vision obstructed.

Just don't forget fresh batteries.

---

[27] *Semi* is a shortened version of semi-trailer, a truck with wheels in the back and supported in the front by a tractor. Semi nothing…it's a full-sized version.

CORC

Coin of the Realm Container - Driving the I requires money. Actually, driving anywhere requires money, but many parts of the I demand Coin of the Realm, and in some places, lots of it. In seventeen miles of Garden State Parkway there are three duty booths, each requiring thirty-five cents[28]. This section of the Garden State is known as the CTL, or Continuous Toll Lane. In a Real Man's Rush Time[29], you can be backed up for the next duty booth within one hundred yards of the one you just left. Thirty-five cent pieces have long been out of circulation, so these takers require two coins minimum. Keeping all that change within easy reach is important. We all know that as you approach a duty booth, people no longer follow any rules of Logic. Coroader lane changing is chaotic at best, so you need to have your money handy in order to keep your eyes on the road. Remember that the person you have been following has dropped their sensibilities and will drive right up to the taker, then start looking for the mysterious combination of seven coins which makes up thirty-five cents. So it pays to have a suitable CORC to hold life's little tokens. Those springy push button jobbers are good, but unless you know how much every combination of coins weighs, you do not know when you are low on which coin without emptying it every time you get near a taker. Planning ahead will fix that, but that's chancy. A shirt with at least two pockets works incredibly well[30].

---

[28] This configuration has been deemed unsafe (finally) by NJDOT and replaced with higher tolls in only one direction...or is that higher tolls in both directions?

[29] *Time* is used here because *hour* is pretty archaic.

[30] Now we are blessed with EZPass and other systems. Just don't forget to pay the bill ahead of time. They'll get your money somehow.

TRASH CAN (TC)

This may seem trivial, but to the Long Distance Traveler, throwing all the empty coffee cups and Roy Paper on the floor is just plain messy, and it means that someone has to clean up that clutter later on after you reach Point B. A plastic bag is all right, but you have to find the opening (possibly in the dark) while using attention on the road. A tough chore at best. A round TC in the front is preferable because a rectangular TC will eventually tip over, spilling contents in places where you do not want contents spilled. You can jam a rectangular TC behind the copilot seat. This makes reaching a TC easy. If you have a bench type seat, then you need something for the front right floor, or, if you have a copilot, put the TC behind the left front seat and the copilot becomes the Sanitation Engineer (SE). If you have an automobile full of people, then designate one person as Sanitary Engineer and make that SE responsible for all trash. Let them decide on the type and location of the TC. Probably someone else's lap.

EXTRANEOUS I MINUTIAE

Serious I voyagers will be on the I under all sorts of weather conditions. Every different condition requires different pieces of hardware or software, but there is a basic list of necessities which should be in the vehicle while on the I. These items are not designed to make the voyage more comfortable, but to assist the autotator in times of need.

Flares or reflectors - should the vehicle become incapacitated for any reason, these will help keep away the inattentive coroaders. They will also attract the attention of the MCs or UMCs, who will then come to your rescue.

Flashlight - An absolute necessity for Dark Side I Voyages. During the daylight hours, a flashlight will aid in searching for that "Ka-tank-a-tank" coming from under the hood.

Blanket - Winter I trips can start out innocently, but can become treacherous. Sudden storms can dump a pile of white on the I and close you down in place. It's good to have a friend in the cold.

Change of clothes - For those roaders who like to tinker, getting oil or roadside crud on your pants or skirt is a way of I life. Always travel in comfortable clothes and have a spare on hand.

Small set of tools - Even if it's just a screwdriver and a couple of wrenches, it will eventually come in handy. Serious I travelers drive a truck with *all* their tools in back. For those autotators who are Craftsman-challenged, carry none, but be ready to rely on the expertise of whoever stops to help.

Fuses - Find out what's in the box and carry at least one of each different kind. Two would be better, because when you replace a fuse the first time, it is going to react the same way the first one did…blow out. Fix the problem first. And make sure you know where the fuse box is.

Fan belt - For very serious voyagers, carrying a fan belt is natural. The problem is that, on newer cars, there is one serpentine fan belt which requires dismantling the entire front end of the automobile. It also costs a small fortune.

Jumper cables - If your battery dies, you can get restarted and at least make it to a garage which doesn't require a down payment.

I, 95

Tire pressure gauge - To see if you are operating under too much pressure. If you are not sure what part pressure plays in your rubber, ask someone who knows and learn how to use this tool.

Once you have designed your perfect space, you're ready to roll. Just remember, you wear your car - it is you. It's like a piece of clothing you put on, so make it comfortable. That's the only way you'll make the trip with any repose. You wouldn't want anyone saying, "I wouldn't be seen dead wearing a car like that."

QUESTION: A cup of Fooder coffee is served at what temperature?

DRIVEAGE

"This is not a right or a left, but a privilege."

AB

The Number One cause of accidents on the I today, by far, is inattention. Autotators will make attempts to dial their cellular phones or perform a sub-par LTT, taking their eyes off of the road for too long a time. Face it, you and they are on the I for one reason, Point B-ing. So why not make your driveage matter? After all, if you remember, we are speaking of an art form. This means using attention.

Here you are, on the throne, foot on the binders, hands on the steerage...put it in gear. Here's where I life starts. Kiss the wife and kindren, drop the PRNDL to Go, squeeze the gooser. You now have the responsibility of safeguarding the lives of thousands of coroaders. The slightly-more-than-one-ton box you are negotiating down the asphalt is a killing machine; although I'm sure Mr. Ford never intended it as such. Every year over forty thousand[31] coroaders lose their lives in traffic accidents on the I. So what to do? Point B is clear in your mind's eye, the vision of the destination - karma... or automobilema. How do you get there? And how do you get there without creating statistics?

---

[31] 1995 statistics stated there were over 43, 000. Exact I statistics are rounded off so no one gets scared. And these are just fatalities.

It's not the route, but the attitude. That's how you get there. It's not as easy as you want to make yourself believe. But you already know that. All your years of experience in steerage are piled up in some remote recess of your cranium, just waiting for that special moment to be brought forth from that faraway hiding place and tested. In a mile of normal driving [32] the average autotator[33] will be forced, without his or her immediate knowledge, to make 250 decisions about the driving program and process over 500 pieces of asphalt related information[34]. A majority of these pieces of information are the mundane "No Parking" signs, but your grey processes these at an incredible speed, without the other half of the brain even having to make any sudden judgments about them. These synapse connections are automatic, sort of the PRNDL of the Mind. But there are many pieces of Triple I which you save, to be added to that vast cavern of knowledge which is sleeping somewhere in the back.

This is the Triple I which has the potential of saving your life or the lives of others, whether they be coroaders or peds[35]. Triple I is filed away in a special section of the grey matter called the UHOH[36]. When it needs to be invoked, Triple I can be called up simply by uttering "Uh oh." This data is categorized as Substantial. It consists of many varied types of information or data. It could be the glance in the rirmir which reveals the overzealous coroader traveling a little too fast, or it may be the "LEFT LANE CLOSED - 3 FEET" sign. All you have to do is see these clues, use attention, and they are automatically filed away for future use, even if that future that is just a millisecond away. And it doesn't cost you a thing.

---

[32] OK, what is normal and who defines it?
[33] OK, who is average and who defines that?
[34] These numbers are totally facetious, but they make a point.
[35] Although peds on the I are not only rare, but illegal.
[36] Pronounced "UHOH".

Not using attention can kill you or a coroader or ped. You or they become a statistic, a number. Especially if you lose it over a holiday[37]. Inattention will allow you to butt the car in front of you, it will allow you to slip unnoticed underneath the semi next to you, it will allow you to cross the dashes and wreak havoc on coroaders. For example, the classic LTT requires incredible amounts of concentration and attention so as to be performed without causing a multicoroader pileup.

Pay attention... why does the phrase use the word "pay"? Attention does not cost a thing, so why do we "pay?" Why not "use", as in "Use attention?" It doesn't cost a thing, but we must use it. It is a requirement, but one for which you pay nothing. The attentive requirements on an autotator are overwhelming. There are not many computers which could handle the amount of data the typical autotator handles in their time in steerage.
So be good at it.

One interesting observation of coroaders is that, for the most part, they are not using attention. They are simply pokin' along, feeling that they are minding their own business and that everyone else should be minding theirs. The problem is that the I is everyone's business. When on the I, you are a part of a single mind, and that mind is singularly bent on one idea: Point B-ing. You cannot mind your own business on the I because by its very nature the I has only one common objective, an objective which everyone becomes a part of when on the I. The only way to achieve true Point B-ing is to cooperate with all the coroaders,

---

[37] Why do we have a morbid curiosity with how many people die on a holiday? I think we are actually being indoctrinated that we are practicing some sort of population control.

to sense their needs and desires, and to manipulate the I accordingly.

On the I there are varying aspects of driveage which require differing levels of attention or concentration. Thinking about these attitudes of driveage (Autotude) will help increase the size of your DIQ. The following list is only a partial compilation of the major headings of subjects which will help you think about what is up down on the I. There are subcategories under these headings which vary with road conditions, the time of day and the Jupiter Effect.

The Roller Coaster Effect

Although it is painfully obvious, it seems that people do not understand advanced automotive physics well enough to grasp the notion that when a mass is descending a hill, it will pick up speed, all other things being equal and the Jupiter Effect is not in force. Now, if "mass" is replaced with "Cadillac", perhaps the concept is easier to comprehend. This is the start of the Roller Coaster Effect. This simply means that once you start downhill, you will eventually go uphill. And since what goes uphill must come downhill, the process is self-reversing. This concept is simply a restatement of the "for every action there is a reaction" belief held by so many eminent physicists. The significance to driveage of this statement is simply "for every downhill there is an uphill."

But something strange takes over many coroaders when going downhill or uphill. It has to do with the fluid surrounding

I, 95

the Cerebellum[38]. When going uphill, this fluid, called "the fluid", recedes to the rear of the cranium, an effect called "backwash", which causes temporary insanity[39]. As long as the vehicle is bound uphill, the insanity continues. This insanity is evidenced by the coroader pushing the gooser all the way to the floorboard of the automobile, thus expending a lot of gasoline to the carburetor or fuel injectors and causing the automobile to increase in speed only slightly. However, over an extended period of time, the automobile will pick up speed and suddenly be quite close to the rear end of the semi in front of it, causing the coroader to suddenly change lanes, the second piece of evidence of temporary insanity. Then they crest the hill.

The same effect is evidenced when going downhill. The fluid rushes to the front of the cranium, again causing insanity for as long as the vehicle is bound downhill. The downhill effect is similar to the uphill effect, except that the speed of *all* vehicles is increasing exponentially. At the bottom of the hill is usually some sort of jam.

The wrench in the Roller Coaster Effect works is autopilot. The problem with autopilot and the Roller Coaster Effect is that not everyone uses autopilot. If everyone was using autopilot, everyone would be speeding up and slowing down at the same rate. Actually, everyone would be maintaining the same rate of speed at the same rate of speed[40]. But not everyone uses autopilot, so some are speeding up and (relatively) some are slowing down. There is no known solution to this problem at this time.

---

[38] A forerunner of the Chevy Celebrity.

[39] Some people incorrectly associate this uphill/downhill behavior with a frontal lobotomy, but on the I it is actually known as a "frontal lobotomobile."

[40] WAY beyond the scope of this book.

SUVs and Other Obstructions

Pickup trucks are popular and necessary in some areas of the country. Those good ol' boys gotta haul stuff[41]. Another of the more popular modes of transportation in the city and the country is the minivan. People haulers. One manufacturer even calls their version an All Purpose Vehicle. It is doubtful that this vehicle will ever haul horse manure from the barn, though. Now, Sport Utility Vehicles (SUVs) are the rage; half truck, half station wagon, half all wheel drive vehicle, these puppies can go anywhere and haul almost anything - a tow hitch is a very common option. But until that SUV gets to the mountains, or until the minivan gets to the mall, you, at some point in your I journey, will be behind it. This presents a special problem.

When following a pickup or a minivan or an SUV, it is not easy to see around it. Some of these vehicles have been seen sporting a bumper sticker stating that "If you can't see my mirrors, I can't see you." Well, thanks very much and we should be more than willing to take the burden of the responsibility for your lack of hind-sight. This attitude demands that you must drive on the dashes so the driver of this overly large vehicle can keep an eye on you. On the I, this simply means leaving a little more room than normal between you and the bozo in front of you because that bozo doesn't give a fig about you, nor do they have rirmir attention[42].

---

[41] There are more pickup trucks in Jackpot, Nevada than in all of New York City.

[42] Not completely different from anal retentiveness.

Alternate Routes (ARs)

In getting from Point A to Point B, one usually makes every attempt to follow the Rule of the Crow. This is also stated as "the shortest distance between two points is a flying crow." This is actually an impossibility. A flying crow, assuming it is flying in a straight line, would have to go through some portion of the earth, thus requiring crow-tunnels and crow-bridges, which have been entirely removed from the budgets of all the states and the Federal government. Simply because of the curvature of the earth, driveage has no straight lines. Everyone has a favorite straight road. There are thousands of them. The record is unknown because no one wants to waste their time finding the straightest road in the United States. Although, in a quick perusal of I mappage, the straightest I seems to be I-94 in North Dakota[43]. But there is still the earth's curvature to deal with. So, if you know that you are not going to go in a straight line, why not create some detours?

Alternate Routes are simply self-directed tours or detours[44]. For those coroaders who are forced to traverse specific Is again and again, ARs are a must. ARs change the scenery, they break monotony, they may save time. Each AR is an individual choice; it is up to each roader to create the AR. Some portions of the I have a multitude of ARs while other sections have no AR at all, unless you consider a 150 mile detour up your traveling alley. There are five times as many ARs as there are Is so only a few ARs will be mentioned here, but the point is to create them and enjoy them. These specific ARs were created for varying reasons, but the they were all used in times of need, be it the need for lack of traffic, or the need for mental readjustment.

---

[43] Requires further research.
[44] The word *detour* still implies a tour.

Some were created out of boredom and were later used for jam avoidance; some were created for jam avoidance and were later used for rest and relaxation. The only requirement for a successful AR creation is the ability to read a map. Mappage is not difficult and should be a requirement on the driving test of all states. If you are unable to negotiate a DeLorme, the creation of ARs is impossible. (See MAPPAGE.)

AR New Jersey I-295 - This is the best route to get by the lower portion of the New Jersey Turnpike. It may not save you any time under normal traffic conditions, but it will save you big dollars. In the north it goes from Exit 7, 5, 4, or 3 off of the Turnpike to the Delaware Memorial Bridge. There is one small hitch ... this could be a very crowded AR near 5 P.M., or whatever is the determinant of the Philadelphia rush time. There is a jag in the road which transverses about one-quarter mile of I-78 and goes to and from the Walt Whitman Bridge and Philadelphia. It can get quite interesting at rush time, although not terminal. The delay is minimal because no one takes that portion of I-295 southbound. During the rush time there are a lot of vehicles on I-295 north of I-78, but they are moving. An added attraction to this AR is that if you get off of I-295 at exit 47A (the Burlington/Mount Holly Route 541 exit, number 5 off of the Turnpike), you can stop and shop at the Burlington Center, a large shopping mall. Gas stations abound on Route 541.

Exit 7 off of the turnpike will lead to route 206 and well-marked signage to lead you between the turnpike and I-295. This is a very short AR, probably about a mile. There are two restaurants[45], one stop light and one gas station, but no places to shop. This is exit 56 off of I-295.

AR Baltimore I-895 - If the Fort McHenry Tunnel on I-95 in Baltimore is in trouble (rare, except during Oriole games or bad driveage), you can take the I-895 I-Can't-Believe-They-Called-It-The Harbor Tunnel. The time is about the same, although I-895 may be only slightly shorter in distance. The reason for this increased time is that the I-895 tunnel is narrower duallane and could present a challenge to the feint if the feint are surrounded by large vehicles or heaps of coroaders. I-895 makes all the appropriate connections.

AR Delaware Route 40 - During Thanksgiving traffic northbound one November there was a 1610 AM warning in Maryland about 20 miles south of the Delaware border forewarning of impending doom at the duty booths in Delaware. Two alternate routes were suggested, both of which ended up on Route 40 in Delaware. Following this road north leads right back into the I just below the Delaware Memorial Bridge. An interesting route, there are many things to do here, include buy liquor on a Sunday and stop for traffic lights every mile. However if the I backs up for the entire state of Delaware[46], this AR is worthwhile.

---

[45] One of which has to be really good. There are always many semis parked there.
[46] This *has* happened.

I, 95

AR Maryland I-295 (for a while) - From the south, you can jump on I-295 through Washington, D.C., just east of the Woodrow Wilson Bridge. Two cautions:

1) do not perform this AR during rush time (Sunday is highly recommended except just prior to or just after Redskin home football games), and

2) make sure you exit left at the north end of this AR in District of Columbia or you will end up with a very difficult and time-consuming return.

I-295 becomes the Baltimore - Washington Expressway (BWE), a cars-only scenic drive with no hope for finding any fooders or worthwhile resters. The only rester is full of phones[47], but no place to "rest" in the I sense of the word. But, fear not, the road is only 30 miles from Washington to Baltimore, so hold onto it for a while. I-295 connects with all the majors approaching Baltimore, so any conjunctions you need to make are there. Many MCs have been spotted on this section of the I.

---

[47] Phoner?

The Block

The I is a great place for football analogies. Well, one, anyway: the Block[48]. The Block involves an inconceivable quantity of mental telepathy between three or more (depending on the laneage) coroaders, usually three who are not using a lot of attention in their environs[49]. These three, again, using telepathy, determine who gets which lane. This determination may seem random to the casual observer, but it follows a carefully calculated blueprint based upon, among many other things, the angle of the setting (or rising) sun and the Jupiter Effect. Other Independent University studies have confirmed that the coroaders in the process of forming the Block are only casually aware of it, if they are aware of anything at all. It has also been validated that 87.7% of the blockers contain coautotators. This is substantial proof that coautotators distract from driveage.

The coroaders involved proceed to perform their Point A to Point B function at or just above the speed limit, in effect, a multi-lane moving jam. While an impressive and complicated maneuver, this creates unthinkable frustration to the trailing coroaders. Blowing has no effect and actually may serve to

---

[48] Fumble, tackle, naked reverse, lateral, interception, touchdown, and many others do not apply. Perhaps the only other one which does apply is *pass*, but not in the sense of throwing anything, except possibly the entire game.

[49] Three coroaders are exemplified here, but the real number is directly proportional to the number of lanes on the particular I being traversed at the time. Circus Maximus blocks are rare, but do occur, especially in Near Jams.

increase the strength of the Block. Still more Independent University studies have attempted to prove that the sound waves emitted by blowers may serve to increase the power of the telepathic waves upon which the blockers are communicating, thus increasing the power which draws these coroaders together and ensuring that their determination to arrive at their respective Bs together is strengthened. These studies have, as yet, proved inconclusive. Blowing is definitely out if these coroaders happen to be wearing badges.

The only solution to breaking a Block is patience. One of the telepathic psychopaths will eventually stop at a fooder or a rester or reach Point B-ing before the others, then their train of thoughtlessness will be broken and the Block will dissolve. Rarely will a blocker change lanes, unless exiting.

Blocks are easy on some roads. The bottom of the New Jersey Turnpike has two lanes south of exit 4. Blocks are plentiful and some are performed quite unintentionally by semis. This is all the more reason to get off at Exit 5 or 7 and head south on 295. The 295 I south of I-78 is a trilane to exit 13, then a duallane to the Delaware Memorial Bridge, but there are not that many coroaders there. I-295 is a great AR.

Buzzing

Buzzing is the act of lane changing on a semi-crowded I (not a Jam, but a traffic condition classified as a Sub-Near Jam) which moves you ahead in a pack. Buzzing can be mentally stimulating. Not only does it advance your position relative to point B, but it also requires careful planning, something we all need to do all of the time in our lives. Buzzing is a sub-art form of driveage. Moving from lane to lane must be done with careful consideration of coroaders because indiscriminate buzzing will cause problems. Buzzing in serious traffic (Near Jams or sub-Near Jams) is verboten. It will only cause reds, and reds at 60 are trouble. Indiscriminate buzzing will also result in a traffic violation if the MCs or UMCs are nearby.

Subtle buzzing, done with panache, will give you a sense of accomplishment. It is mentally stimulating to know you have outsmarted most of the pack, now far behind you. Bad buzzing, usually resulting in driving into a cave (see LANEAGE), is frustrating and will cause ulcers, a full bladder, and spilled coffee. Good buzzing is rewarding. Buzzing left is preferred, but buzzing right is a requirement when there is a middle mushroom and a coroader coming up on the left. Extreme caution must be exercised when buzzing right on a semi. This move must be accomplished quickly and with care. If the particular semi being buzzed has a skull and crossbones pointing to the right, do not buzz right. Use careful attention on semis, they are very important and dangerous when wounded.

The real challenge for the buzzer is the middle mushroom / poker combination. This will test the buzzer's abilities and nerves.

Cleaning the Glass

At some point in the game you will find a need to clean your windshield. It is a seemingly unimportant maneuver which can be very satisfying ("Hey! I can see!") and will result in improved Quarter Up vision down the I. This action, like all others involved in the art of driving, must be planned somewhat in advance, but take heart, it consists of only two steps.

I, 95

Step One: Make sure you have a full jug of the Blue. This is the "advance planning" stage of this action, but it is simple enough. The commercial Blue you can purchase at the checkout lane of any self-respecting store is sufficient, and pre-mixed. You can make your own, but if you do not create the proper proportion of water and methyl alcohol (or whatever that toxic waste is), one of two things will happen:

1) It will freeze in the container under the hood. This will not be good because on the newer autos removal of the Bluejug requires removal of the engine and a 3/4 tine Torsten/Blatfell wrench;
2) The mixture you make will cause your windshield to melt.

Step Two: Infinitely more fun than Step One. You're on the I doing 60 or 65. There are many other coroaders at less than 6 dashes. Now is the time to clean the glass. So, you press the button, pull the stick, turn the knob... just perform whatever action necessary to start the Blue oozing over the glass. This action will cover your windshield with the Blue and require turning on the wipes; but at 60 to 65 miles per hour, the spraying Blue dispersed by the wipes will cover not only your windshield but much of the resulting spray will hit the coroader behind you. This will result in impaired vision for that coroader, requiring him or her to perform the same function you just performed. The result is inevitable: everyone in this lane of traffic will have clean windshields. This phenomenon is known as I-wash. There is one danger to all this, though. Under certain lighting conditions, if the coroader behind you has an empty Bluejug, they will panic when they see a wave of the Blue heading their way and cause lots of reds behind them. Unfortunately there is no way to know the status of a tailgater's Bluejug[50].

This whole performance, of course, assumes that every coroader in your lane has performed Step One with the same fanaticism that you have. One dry Bluejug will ruin it for everyone. Pray for rain.

Dash Coefficient

To stay out of the compost of accidentdom, coroaders need to pace themselves. In New York and the New Jersey portion of New York, the game they play seems to be to stay as close as possible to the auto in front of them. It's sort of a 60 mile per hour jam. But when one autotator lets off the gooser, the behinder has to go red. Of course, this chain reacts to all others, the road goes red, and suddenly the speed drops to 25 miles per hour or so. In the meantime, the lead horse is off again, but the damage is already done: Jam. Unless a good dash coefficient is maintained, this action will result in a jam every time.

So maintain a good Dash Coefficient! The typical I dash[51] is ten feet long, five inches wide and separated thirty feet from the

---

[50] One wonderful benefit of having the ability to spray the Blue beyond the limits of one's windshield is the capability to now defend one's rear bumper. If you are being threatened from the rear, you can use the Blue to warn the perpetrator to back off. Simply perform the above steps. The result is that the tailgater will let off the gas and increase the space between you and them. This is known as Blueshooting.

[51] Dashes have very colorful names, depending who you are talking to. Their real names are Skip Lines, but depending where they are and how they are configured, they can be called Puppy Feet or Elephant Tracks.

I, 95

adjacent dash[52]. This makes the dash-to-dash distance forty feet. This is about the necessary distance required at twenty miles per hour to keep you from butting, should the auto in front of you go pure red[53]. So, to maintain TE (Traffic Equilibrium), you should allow one dash per twenty miles per hour of speed, the Dash Coefficient. How do you do this without taking your full attention off of the road? Since the dashes do not have numbers on them, it needs a little practice, but it is not that hard. The reason the dashes are so big is to allow you to see them out of the corner of your eye. Practice this the next time you are on the road. Just concentrate out of the corner of your eye. You can see them. Set a starting point, easily done by shouting "NOW!" at the top of your lungs. When you do this, you determine the dash which has just passed the rear bumper of the roader in front of you. Keeping your eye on that dash, you count the dashes you pass with your front bumper. When the dash you have been watching passes your bumper, you have the dash count between you and the roader in front of you. Multiplying quickly by forty feet (the dash factor) you can determine the exact distance

---

[52] Much of this information was obtained from the VDOT (Virginia, not Vermont) and the Maryland Transportation Authority. It is valid for Virginia, Maryland and many other states. However, careful observation has determined that some DOTs do one of two things when dashing; 1) they don't have lots of paint so they allow for more feet between dashes (Delaware) or, 2) they have lots of paint so they make the dashes longer and decrease the Interdash Gap (Garden State Parkway).

[53] Pure red is the locking up of the tires. On ABS equipped vehicles, there is no smoke to indicate that the vehicle is coming to a rather quick stop.

between vehicles, thus coming to the inevitable conclusion that you need to either 1) slow down, or 2) speed up[54].

If you slow down, inevitably, someone will say "Yeah, but then someone will cut in front of me." So? Let that person hit the person in front of them. You don't need to be standing on the side of the road swapping insurance papers. You know that someone on the other side of the I will be rubbernecking.

Positions

In the heyday of Citizen's Band radio, coroaders (and anyone else who happened to hear *Convoy!* on the radio) became aware of a colorful lingo used by CBers to describe many different kinds of traveling situations. That language seems to have faded into the past somewhat, but remnants survive.

When on the I, position is important: location, location, location. There is a need for a language describing the relative positions of your vehicle in its journey between points. To this end, the following should be used in describing any eventualities on the I. (I promise not to use them again.)

Tailgunner - the last car in the pack. A good position to be in for planning a buzz. The tailgunner position gives you a very good perspective on the coroaders up ahead.

Lead Horse - the first car in the pack. In this position it is absolutely necessary to have one's eyes on the rirmir. A very challenged position.

---

[54] For those mathematically challenged, one dash is 40 feet, two dashes are 80 feet, three dashes are 120 feet,... get a calculator with big numbers and a big display and keep it in your vehicle.

I, 95

Bridging the Gap - being in a position between two packs or blocks. This could be a dangerous position because radar guns will pick you out easily.

Buzzing the Pack - the action necessary to move from tailgunner to lead horse. This usually takes time (depending on the size of the pack) and can be frustrating to accomplish. Use patience and care. In theory, it is impossible to buzz a block, although with the carefully timed blinking of the high beams and the patience of Job, it can be accomplished.

Flotsam and Jetsam

Yes, Virginia, there is a difference, although as you travel the I most of what you see is the black pieces of vulcanized rubber from the recap off of that semi that went by here a half-hour ago. Jetsam is the stuff which is discarded intentionally, originally intended to mean the stuff thrown off of a ship at sea to lighten the load in a time of distress, i.e., the ship is sinking. Flotsam is the stuff which comes after the ship has sunk, the stuff not intended to get in anyone's way, but which shows up all the same. So the pieces of recap littering the I is definitely flotsam. The jetsam is inexcusable. A roader can be fined heavily for jetsam on the I. We will assume here that the flotsam is flotsam and we are all grown up enough not to create jetsam.

On a long-ago trip down the I, my very young children entertained themselves by propelling Tupperware Lid projectiles out of the vent window of the Toyota. Unfortunately, us adults did not discern the problem for miles. Tupperware jetsam.

Coming across flotsam can be a real driving experience, especially if you do not maintain proper dash coefficience. One great reason for maintaining a good dash coefficient is to keep an eye on the movements of the vehicle directly in front of you as he or she tries to steer clear of the paper-bag-which-doesn't-move-in-the-wind flotsam. Small flotsam can be positioned to glide underneath the vehicle, but larger chunks in the middle of the lane are dangerous. Roaders will go to many lengths (with the notable exception of stopping to pick it up) to avoid flotsam, and you had better be ready when it comes your way.

It is comical to watch the Cadillac Eldorado drive over the plastic bag and have the bag attach itself to the undercarriage. You feel like yelling, "Hey Lady! Your slip is showing!"

I, 95

QUESTION: How much paint does it take to paint a one mile long solid stripe on the I?

I GAMES

"An I mind is a terrible thing to waste"

AB

Long voyages on the I can be particularly lonely. Even with the various means of communications available, entertainment is minimal. Television is out, except for the coautotators of the rich and famous, and even though singing along with your favorite group or conducting your favorite orchestra is enjoyable, there is still that gnawing sensation that there must be something to do, a game to play. To this end, included here are some of the games autotators play.

Alphabet Soup/Cutthroat Soup

This is a great game. I have played this not only with my family, but also solo and it does help pass the time. The object of the game is to get all the letters of the alphabet, in order. If you attempt to get them out of order, you will invariably lose your place. Anything outside your space is fair game. If playing with more than one person, Cutthroat Soup requires that everyone keep track of how many letters they get, first to twenty-six wins. This is great in states with lots of antique shoppes and pizza palaces, but can be a challenge, for example, on the southern portion of the New Jersey Turnpike where there is one sign every 22 miles. There are no antique shoppes in New Jersey.

I, 95

You have to rely on antique semis and those are few and far between. Maine is a great state for Antiques. Every state has Exits. This game has a definite end. One Alphabet Soup game was completed in 25 miles in Virginia. The current, unofficial record is 24 out of 26 at a backed up duty booth in Delaware. Actually, the game was played over the entire state of Delaware, but the traffic jam for the duty booth *was* the entire state. Someone will soon be an official scorekeeper.

Numbers

This is a variation of Alphabet Soup which is played with, oddly enough, numbers. Simply start at one and go[55]. This game has no end. My daughter and I (the only ones left counting) are up to 750 after two and a half years. Numbers can be separated by dashes, periods, etc., the only rule is that they must be consecutive. You will find that single digits are a breeze (after all, there are only 9 of them, ten if you're a hardliner), double digits are more of a challenge, and triple digits are downright frustrating. This is a life challenge. Excruciating pain ensues when you are looking for the number 243 and you see 244 three times. The numbers can come in bunches. The light poles on the Tappan Zee Bridge are all numbered. The New Jersey Turnpike (as most major Is in New Jersey) has mile markers every tenth of a mile, but they are consecutive only heading north and east. The southbounder or westbounder has only one shot to get large numbers. And no U-turns allowed.

---

[55] Hardliners start at zero.

States

Simple, but entertaining. You just have to find as many different state license plates as you can. This game, unfortunately, requires either incredible memory powers or a copilot or co-autotator to take notes, but it keeps you abreast of the latest models of license plates[56]. There are many states which now offer specialty plates for all sorts of causes, some very worthy, but most just plain vain.

Leapfrog

A driving game, but don't get carried away. Pick a car going about the same speed you are, then follow them for a while. The amount of time depends on the length of the road you are on and the phase of the moon, and throwing in the Jupiter Effect doesn't hurt. Then pass them and pull in front. Maintain enough speed to keep them behind for a while. Then slow down and allow them to pass you. Keep this up long enough to either make them very angry or realize that they have been drawn into the game. Then the fun begins. Multiple lane leapfrog can be challenging and entertaining. Just don't lose track of other coroaders. You two are not the only autotators.

---

[56] Virginia takes the honors for that: there are over 300 different styles of license plate available there. All you need for your own special vanity plate is 150 people and a logo.

I, 95

QUESTION: Counting only single style plates, how many plates could you find on the I?

JAMS

"Into I life a little jam must fall."

AB

Traffic jams are a part of I life. If you are going to enjoy the I, you will eventually be a part of a jam. The causes of a jam vary as widely as the weather. Jams can be caused by accidents, bubbles, bubblestops, rubbernecking, bad driveage, or a host of other idiocies. At some point in your I life you will be in a jam. And it will cost you time. Bowditch's First.

Accidents are the number one cause of jams. It only takes two to dance the Mango[57], and with so many vehicles on the I, only one little slip of that attention button will lock up the I faster than a speeding Buick. Participants of fender-benders typically stop where they are, assess the damage in place, then pull over to the side to swap papers. But the jam is already in progress, and usually before the two or more participants come to a complete stop. That's when the fun begins. More serious accidents usually stay in place until the Officials arrive.

Compost happens. That's the ecological long range view of things[58]. All us I voyagers run across them eventually ... accidents. An accident may be the cause of the current jam you are enjoying. Hopefully we do not become part of them, but are

---

[57] Mangle-Tango.
[58] Forrest Gump and an untold number of bumper stickers have pointed out the short term four letter version of that.

I, 95

only passing them by. With a little attention, no one has to be involved. It is always amazing that accident rubbernecking seems to cause most jams[59]. What are these coroaders trying to see? Blood? Great. Then what? A tale to tell?

"Man, I was driven' up 95 and there was this accident, and, man, there was all this blood and car parts everywhere!"

If you want blood and car parts, stay home and watch Arnold Swartzennegger movies. If you are afforded the opportunity of taping the accident, you can replay it when all your friends are over. A crash party. So, how do you tape an accident? The obvious solution is portable grandstands.

Portable grandstands can be brought in by a special police truck or private or police helicopter to the scene of any accident. They could even be delivered by specially equipped multi-purpose ambulances. There could be a special police unit which would set up the grandstands and sell tickets. There could even be a franchise ... *Roadkill and Wreckage, Inc.* The typical roader can then pull off of the I into a designated parking area, stop for a rest, pay an entrance fee, and watch as the ambulance personnel pull the mangled autotator from the wreckage. Videotaping is allowed and encouraged. If someone gets kicked in the groin you can send the tape to America's Funniest Home Videos. The proceeds from the entrance fee can be used to defray the costs of the accidents, because, as we all know, all our insurance rates will rise because the people involved in the accident did not have insurance. USE ATTENTION!

Bubbles are great for jamming. On a dull day they will do the speed limit in any lane they please. Pass them only if you're feeling frisky. Technically, if you are doing fifty-six miles per hour in a fifty-five mile per hour zone, you are breaking the law.

---

[59] The cause of a rubberjam doesn't even have to be an accident, it could simply be a breakdown.

That's where the word "limit" comes into effect. But most scofflaws figure that seven miles per hour over the limit is all right and acceptable, so 62 miles per hour is okay. Where the scofflaws get this information is a mystery, but the seven mile per hour figure seems to be universal. Well, if Smokey Bear is feeling out-of-sorts, take your own chances. He's moving along the I at fifty-five miles per hour, feeling just fine at how he is upholding the law. Hey, if given the opportunity, the average autotator would too. Imagine being paid to drive at fifty-five miles per hour and collect money from people who pass you. Great job!

Bubblestops will cause jams, albeit temporarily. No one wants to speed past a bubble which has already determined that it is his day to refill the coffers of the state treasury. Passing a bubblestop at more than five miles per hour over the limit is risky because you do not know how many friends this bubble has just down the road, and *he* has the radio. So you slow down because everyone in front of you has gone red and you ease past the bubblestop at the speed limit and everyone behind you has already gone red. But when you get just out of range, hit the gooser. No one knows for sure just what this distance is, the "out of range" distance. So everyone makes an educated guess and prays they have made the right decision. It is rare for a trooper to drop one bubblestop for another of the same value. But you never know just how close he or she is to ticket completion.

Bad driveage can be a serious jammer. Jam-causing bad driveage can be anything from lefties to weavers, those people who have no conception of white lineage. It can be an exciting experience to attempt to pass these people. Typically they are near or past license retirement age. These coroaders, unfortunately, have a distorted concept of I driveage. They feel that they are alone on the I and owe nothing to no one, having

I, 95

already settled all their debts. All the rest of the coroaders have to compensate for their shortcomings. Most of the time, coroaders are successful at this compensation, but that one time where bad driveage meets bad driveage can be devastating.

Perhaps the most frustrating cause of jams on the I is rubbernecking. The term "rubbernecking" applies, of course, to autotators who turn their heads and necks and shoulders and torsos as they autotate in a usually vain attempt to catch a glimpse of the carnage which they secretly hope has occurred. Rubbernecking applies to either direction of the I near the accident. If the cause is in the Northbound lanes, not only do the Northbound lanes come to a standstill, but also the Southbound lanes because of the typical coroader fascination with the hideous and fender-bent. For some gruesome reason, most coroaders cannot keep their eyes off of the gore or the twisted metal. If there is a chance of seeing blood or a mangled Mercury, they will slow down. The more flashing lights there are, the slower they will go. There is no way to avoid rubberneckers because it only takes one to slow the entire I. That person puts all their attention to the accident or bubblestop and completely forgets that their primary I function is to maintain sanity on their side of the I. As they gaze upon the possible carnage, they become weavers, they slow down, they lose control. and you, behind them by a foot or a mile, have to react to their stupidity. Let's jam.

QUESTION: Why do we park on driveways and drive on parkways?

I POLICE

"They serve to protect and remind."

AB

There are so many terms applied to these gentle men and women of the State Highway Patrols and their vehicles that the terminology has become cumbersome. Cops, Bears, Smokies, Bubble Gum Machines, Fuzz, Bubbles, MCs, UMCs, the list goes on and on and contains names not proper to be printed here[60]. But these public servants are there to remind us that without rules and enforcement, life on the I would be chaotic at best and good driveage would be unattainable.

What would life be like without those state troopers keeping everyone under 80 miles per hour? Well, you, for one, should be thankful. If everyone out there were doing 90 mph, something would give. There would be the mushroom, or the tire flotsam from the semi that went by this spot an hour ago. The Troopers have a tendency to remind us that the objective of the game is not to see how long you can keep the speedo pegged before you hit something, but that it really is a pleasure to get there in one piece. And they have such fast cars and neat uniforms.

They use MCs and UMCs. Marked Cars are, of course, much easier to pick out in a crowd moving up behind you, but

---

[60] It would be interesting to discuss the origins of these words. See *The Zenistic Implications of Naming Police and Their Vehicles.*

I, 95

the UnMarked Cars will get you every time[61]. Some states use MCs exclusively, but these are rarer and rarer. Most states now have UMCs primarily, and MCs to just hide in the bushes and have a cup of joe, providing an effective jam. Virginia even has unmarked Vans.

"Hey, honey, there's some family in a van trying to pull us over...let's show 'em what this car can do!"

Finding a hiding place has become a real challenge for the Bubbles. The stereotypical behind-the-billboard statie is a thing of the past, primarily thanks to all the First Ladies who have lobbied so hard to make our travels infinitely more boring by removing all the billboards from the side of the road. No more reading while you're driving. Sure the countryside is prettier what with all the wild flowers planted in the medians, but after about 100 miles of pansies it's so boring. GIMME A BILLBOARD! So without the billboards, where do the ladies and gents with the neat hats go?

The advent of the billboardless countryside has spawned median strips with flowerbeds and botanical eruptions. Yes, it is pleasing to look at, and it may afford the crafty cop a neat place to hide. Sitting amongst the blooms with a handful of antihistamine pills, the Trooper keeps his radar gun aimed mercilessly down the I. One enterprising Statie long ago tried this, but the lawn had not been mowed in a while and the heat from the catalytic converter actually started a grass fire. That's an awful thing to have to confess to.

Then there is the "Authorized Vehicle Only" U-turn lane[62]. This area can be a little more exposed than the flower bed

---

[61] Recent trends in car-jackings by unofficial UMCs has spurred the return to the MC. A wonderful comment on the times.

[62] Has anyone asked to see the piece of paper which authorizes the Troopers to use that lane? I doubt it.

I, 95

station, but some of them are pretty well covered over with trees. Imagine what conversation could be going on when you see two of them in there...

"Hey Billy Joe, how ya doin?"

"Fine Billy Bob, and you?"

"OK. Hey didja see that tractor trailer that overturned down by exit 25?"

"Yeah! That was somethin'! Hell, I wouldn't be caught dead near that. I think it was hazardous waste. I Uied immediately and scared the daylights out of a family from Nebraska! You shoulda seen the looks on their faces!"

"Neat!"

Typical cop/donut jokes will be omitted here, but if you are anywhere near the Stafford exit on I-95 in Virginia, it is worth getting off, heading east for a very short AR and looking for the police station on the north side of the road. Well worth it.

One of my nicest, unique experiences heading north on the I in Maryland was watching a caravan of fifteen MCs in row. There was no clue as to where they came from or where they were going. Everyone heading south about that time was doing just about the speed limit. The thing that made it so funny was that there was a 16th MC hanging back about a quarter of a mile from the main caravan. Just when you thought the 70's were safe.

63

I, 95

On I-95 in Maryland at about Mile Marker 101 there is a group of I maintenance buildings. Until recently, the I Police in Maryland maintained a vehicle parked in the front yard of one of these buildings, clearly in the view of roaders on the I. To make this vehicle as authentic as possible, the Maryland I Police installed a dummy ("Maryland Max") behind the wheel, complete with Trooper hat and mean look[63]. This, one can only assume, was intended to slow people down as they passed this building, thinking that they were about to be radared into submission. The dummy had to have been a failed CPR dummy, which means that instead of being just dead, it could not even be resuscitated. In the winter of 1995-1996 the vehicle and Maryland Max were removed from in front of the building. The removal was probably due to the fact that there were eighteen inches of snow on the ground and the vehicle. If Maryland Max had been left there, everyone would have wondered why a State Trooper would be in his vehicle in the middle of the winter with the engine not running. Who knows? Maybe the roaders would have taken pity on Maryland Max and stopped to leave coffee and doughnuts.

Maryland Max is aided conveniently by radar. That invisible "gotcha" that all state and local troopers utilize to catch you in the act of performing some incredibly illegal act. So the United States public is exposed to radar detectors for sale[64], then the police develop radar undetectable to the average radar detector. So the public is exposed to more sophisticated radar detectors. Now we will pay two hundred dollars to avoid a fifty dollar fine.

---

[63] The "mean look" was difficult to discern at 65 miles per hour, but you know it had to be there.

[64] Except in Virginia and a few other locations, where use of a radar detector is illegal and subject to confiscation. What do they do with all the radar detectors they confiscate? Sell them in Maryland.

I, 95

Many police forces still use helicopters or airplanes to determine who is speeding. Those large white lines perpendicular to the highway are the start and stop points which are used to time the vehicle from the air. If you see a sign which states that your vehicle speed is being monitored from some sort of aircraft, just pass one of these lines and jam on your brakes for a half a second. This should be enough to blow the average that the aircraft is determined to assign to you.

I, 95

QUESTION: How many miles per year does the average Maryland State Police vehicle (bubble) go in a year?

SIGNAGE

"I know it's along here somewhere."

AB

There is an art to reading and interpreting typical I signage. We've all grown accustomed to quintessential "Speed Limit," "Wrong Way" and "No U-turn" signs. Most of us feel that it can't be much harder than that. Well, imagine that your duty booth coin of the realm is going to a department which just makes up signage. An entire division of the DOT is dedicated to the wording and location of large and small informative and demanding signage. This department, like any other department, conducts committee meetings dedicated to the wording of signage. Tapes of the minutes of the meetings are usually destroyed because no one wants to leak any information concerning the arguments which ensue about whether or not to use the words "Speed Limit" or "Warp Factor Maximum." These Wording Meetings are usually amicable. The Locations Meetings usually break out in fist fights.

Signage is broken down into four main categories: Mandatory ("Speed Limit"), Warning ("Beware of Ogres in Tunnel"), Informational ("Scenic Overview", Gas-Food-Lodging), and Directional (Exit and Distances). There are numerous sub-categories of these majors, but they are inconsequential, and as you are motivating down the I, they are not very interesting to think about.

I, 95

Mandatory Signage

These are primarily "Speed Limit" signs. This information, if ignored, will result in penalties. Sort of like cross-checking in a hockey game. Besides "Speed Limit," these include "All Traffic Must Exit," "Bridge Out Ahead," "Stop for Sobriety Check," and "Do Not Enter."

Warning Signage

These can be ignored under most circumstances. "Speed Limit" signs in yellow are a recommended limit, not a mandate. Use this signage to adjust to road conditions. "Slippery When Wet" is a good example. In Holland, yellow signage picturing a car driving into a body of water is a good indication that you should at least slow down. This signage includes recommended Speed Limits, "Kangaroo Crossings", "Loose Gravel" and "Dangerous Cross Winds" or "X-Winds," if you can figure out what "X" winds are[65].

Informational Signage

If your journey down the I is for pleasure, use attention to these brown or blue signs. They indicate places of interest or local color. These include "Rest Area," "Hospital," "The Great Pumpkin Patch," or some historic event which occurred on this spot hundreds of years ago[66]. This is great if you're a history buff, but if you're just trying to avoid slipping under the wheels

---

[65] Seems there should be Y-Winds, too. If X-winds are blowing across your line of travel, then Y-winds should make your trip either longer or shorter.

[66] Civil War Battle sites are in Blue and Grey.

of a semi, an informational sign is just an annoyance. They make you think you're missing something. Which you will.

Directional Signage

These green signs simply tell you that you have just passed the exit you wanted or how far you have to travel in this incredible jam. They are green. They are so green that if you have the sun reflect off of them at the right angle, you can see leprechauns.

The signs which are important are either too small to read or are on the wrong side of the I. You're leapfrogging and you're in the left lane of a trilane. There's a semi in the right lane that is blocking signage that says "Bear in Bushes - 1/4 mile." Great. The Locations Committee got you on that one. Bowditch's Second states that important signage will be displayed improminantly or out of sight. Important (mandatory) signage will not be displayed where you will see it. (The Locations Committee strikes again.) A good example of this is off the I, but appropriate nonetheless. At National Airport in Washington, D.C., the one square foot "Rental Car Return" sign with left pointing arrow is at knee level in the right lane of an always congested roadway. So you have to go round again and cross two lanes of intense, horn-honking traffic to get to where you want to be. On the I, looking ahead is mandatory. Always be Quarter Up, checking for color-coded signage.

Portasignage

Interpreting color-coded signage should be second nature to the seasoned I voyager. Now, to keep things lively, DOTs have started using portable signage. These are the Rent-a-Signs operated by a generator which is part of the signage and can be

I, 95

programmed to display any message the DOT deems fit. "Have a nice day" is pretty blasé now, but the information contained on these beauties can be important. The more is flashes, the more important it is. Bowditch's Third. Portasignage is used primarily to warn of impending construction, but usage for other reasons is growing. Imagine the Portasignage Message Committee debates on that! The older version of the portasigns usually had a bulb or two out, or a flipper that didn't flip and the message could be confusing. Instead of warning of impending disaster, a portasign may read "Bride Out Ahead" and you'll smile as you recall your honeymoon and go off into dreamile not realizing that your wheels just left terra firma.

Bowditch's Third states that anything that flashes has to be important. This dates back to the 9th Century and the invention of gunpowder. That was important. The initial discovery surely surprised Oh Poo, the inventor. He realized (quickly) how important that flash was. Now, centuries later, we have flashing portasignage and non-portasignage that indicate situations to which we should pay heed, no matter how trivial they seem. The flashing may be a single yellow light or a whole DOT truck lit up with enough wattage to signal Jupiter that there is intelligent life on this planet. The flashers are usually yellow, use attention. Red flashers are rare, but inevitably indicate complete shutdown of whatever systems are currently in place. Blue flashers are MCs[67].

Interpreting signage on the I can be challenging, but only if you can see it and have enough time to read it. On the Washington, D.C. Beltway (in Maryland) there is a sign in the median that asks the question "Fender Bender?" then gives instructions as to how you should pull out of the way of oncoming traffic and slug it out. It is very difficult to read at 60

---

[67] It is illegal in Virginia to have any blue lights on your vehicle. Good thing MCs can't drive in a K-Mart.

miles per hour. This signage is in yellow, blue and white so it is, by design, very confusing. But what if you are from another country or planet? It assumes you know what a fender bender is. Foreign guitar players are at a special disadvantage. They may just obey the signage, pull over and start jamming on the side of the beltway. I have seen traffic on the beltway stop for all sorts of things, but that would be a new one.

At the entrances to the New Jersey Turnpike, the rules are posted. This signage contains the entire rules and regulations of driving on the turnpike. It is a large sign with multiple columns of fine print. There is usually no place to pull over and read it, yet, if you violate those rules, you can be sure that the Mountie is going to say, "Well, sir [or ma'am], the rules are posted. Didn't you read them?"

So interpretation is important. How do you really translate all the signage? Here are some typical signs and their *real* meanings, not what history has dictated to all us coroaders:

Speed Limit   How fast your car will go given all the gasoline you can supply. If you beat the indicated number for an extended period of time, you win a prize.

Dangerous X-Winds   Lethal alien flatulence

Yield   Go as fast as you can and ignore all coroaders.

Hazmat Carriers Use Right Two Lanes[68]   Stay left

---

[68] No where in the driving instruction books does it define what a "HAZMAT" is. The various DOTs assume that you and the HAZMAT driver already know.

I, 95

Authorized Vehicles Only   Okay to drive here if your car has written anything lately.

Many Is now have exits labeled A and B. This signage has actually been around for a long time since I designers realized that a majority of coroaders do not know whether they want to get off at the North, East, South, or West exit. And, unless indicated to them, many autotators do not know the direction in which they are traveling. Designers place the names of cities or large towns on signage in the hopes that roaders will remember that Point B lies near that location, but experience has proven that this is not only futile, but inaccurate. To attempt to alleviate the stress induced when the autotators get off the I, find themselves heading in the wrong direction and have to execute a more than likely illegal, unauthorized U-turn, the various State Signage Committees simply called the exits A and B. This change was also the result of conservation efforts since it is more economical to use two letters instead of four. But is there a real rhyme or reason for the A and B designations, or are the A and B exits chosen at random?

The answer is Yes, with qualifications. Independent University study has proven that Exit A goes East or South, and that, as a natural result, Exit B goes North or West. This is all predetermined by the current direction of your navigation. There is no easy mnemonic to remember this, like "HOMES" or "All Good Girls Go Green by Eighteen" or something like that. Unless you can deal with SEA (South or East is A, or, Someone Eats Anchovies) and WNB (West or North is B, or, Why Not Boogie?), there is no easy answer. There are many exceptions to this, notably in New Jersey. Exit 154 on the Garden State Parkway has two parts, but they are not labeled A and B, they are labeled Exit 154 and Exit 154P. Wonderful. Unless you live

I, 95

in Paterson, this is Greek. Someone from Pennsylvania may take Exit 154P thinking they are on their way to Punxsutawney to see Phil. What a surprise. Paterson is nothing like Punxsutawney.

    Delaware seems to bear out the SEA/WNB dilemma, as does Virginia. The SEA/WNB mnemonic is consistent. The solution is to have a compass on board. That way you will know which direction you are headed, and which way to turn to head for a specific direction. But then you must have the knowledge that Point B is West, North, or whatever, and there is the case for on-board computers. The closest thing we have available now is the larger vehicles with the compass built into the inside rirmir. We can only hope it's big enough to see, and lit up at night.

I, 95

QUESTION: What does red signage mean?

ETIQUETTE and DISETIQUETTE

"Do unto others, always."

AB

We all end up on the I at some point, be it early in life or two days later. When we do end up on it, we want to be treated with all the respect and courtesy due us. The "Do Unto Others" proverb hits home on the I. Nothing annoys coroaders more than being treated disrespectfully by ANYONE else on the I. Disrespect (or disetiquette) is due to a number of things. Stupidity, forgetfulness, and bad design are just a few of these. Stupidity in bad driveage, forgetfulness in leaving high beams on at night (Beamers), bad design in those idiotic, usually misdirected "driving lights." Etiquette means we all get to Point B in a good mood, satisfied that we accomplished what we set out to do, not having caused or been involved in a major jam in the process. If we were all polite out there on the I, much Point B-ing would be accomplished without the aggravation of jams or unnecessary honking. There are a few major categories of etiquette and disetiquette which should make us all aware of each other, and our own mis-habits[69] on the I.

---

[69] A Mis-habit is not a bad habit, but not a good habit. But it leans closer to bad than good.

LEFTIES - Lefties use the left lane as their personal driveage room. We have all seen coroaders pull onto the I and, for no apparent reason, make a bee-line for the left lane[70]. Then, when someone moving more rapidly than the Leftie comes along, they sit there, forcing the more rapidly moving vehicle to pass on the right, probably causing travail among pokers. Historically, the left lane is the passing lane. European autotators learn quickly to stay to the right. Bowditch's Fourth. Lefties think this lane is the fastest, so they go there, and they stay there.

So what is the purpose of bee-lining to the left lane? It seems that many people are inflicted with an I infection called Leftism. The symptom, of course, is driving in the left lane for no good reason, especially any reason relating to passing another vehicle. Ninety-nine percent of the coroaders afflicted with Leftism are also afflicted with co-autotation. Leftism is curable, but it must be caught in its incipience, especially by MCs. However, MCs are the remaining one percent. On Mid-Atlantic I-95, Leftism can be found in coroaders primarily from New York, Pennsylvania, and Virginia, although every state has its fair share.

LEFFOOTS - A derivative of Leftism is a condition known as "Leffoot." Leffoots are found to drive with their left foot on the brake pedal, thus keeping their brake lights on constantly. As a result, trailing coroaders never know when the leffoot will come to a stop, or is attempting to slow down. Extreme caution must be exercised when following a leffoot. A mild case of leffoot is evidenced by a condition known as "brake dancing." Just enough pressure is exerted on the brake pedal to cause the

---

[70] Not quite sure what a bee-line (B-line?) is, but it may have something to do with a Buick.

tail lights to blink on and off. This is especially aggravating to trailing coroaders since it seems, at times, that the brake dancer is almost in control of their reasoning.

BEAMERS[71] - Coroaders (remember: this is in the Stupid Category) sometimes leave their high beams on while on the I at night. Why? Automotive Engineers designed a wonderfully soothing blue light into the cluster to indicate to the autotator that the incredibly intense (especially in the Halogen Age) lights on the front of the auto are engaged. To the normal autotator, the soothing blue is a good indicator that he or she is supplying an incredible amount of light into either the 1) oncoming vehicles or 2) the rirmirs of the vehicles in front of you. Large, old pickup trucks have unadjustable right and left outside rirmirs. These rirmirs attract most of the light generated by high beams[72]. There is an affliction (rare) amongst coroaders called Blueblindness, a color blindness wherein blue lights are indiscernible. These autotators do not shop at K-Mart, nor do they see or care that their high beams are on and blinding you. A majority of vehicles are now equipped with outside rirmirs on the right side which contain the statement "Objects In Mirror Are Closer Than They Appear." Good Warning. However, the Beamer does not see the warning that reads "Objects in mirror appear much much brighter than they are." They suffer from Blueblindness.

Beamers make you wish you had a device similar to the one in the old Hertz or Avis advertisement which cut the car in half. Maybe someday there will be a device on the market which will allow you to electronically disable the beamer. Aim, point and

---

[71] Not to be confused with Beemers, or Bummers.
[72] The so-called "White Hole" effect.

I, 95

click so that all of the electronics on the beamer's automobile simply stop working.

DRIVING LIGHTS - These lights also fall into the Idiot Light category. No one is quite sure what the purpose of these driving lights is. If they are driving lights, what are the other ones?[73] Interestingly enough, these driving lights only come on when the low beams are on, not when the high beams are illuminated. So what are they for? Only to blind coroaders or to identify roadkill after dark with oncoming traffic. Most of these driving lights are misaligned or maladjusted so that instead of picking up the poor possum and making it road kill, they shine up into the eyes of the oncomer. Useless.

OTHER LIGHTS IN GENERAL - When people purchase or lease their vehicle, they demand that everything be in perfect working condition. They will return that brand new vehicle simply because a light is non-functional. So why do these same people not care a fig when a light burns out later on in the vehicle's life? At night on the I being followed by a pediddle is disconcerting. It is difficult to tell if you're being followed by a motorcycle or a vehicle real close to you with one light out. Depth perception is difficult. Discerning the speed of that lights-out vehicle is also difficult. The same is true of elddideps. Depth perception as you approach an elddidep is also difficult. Until your headlights pick up reflective surfaces, you cannot tell how far away that elddidep is.

---

[73] Yes, there are Parking Lights, but these are not quite so intense. And most parked cars do not use these lights. Parking lights are only used as signaling devices in B movies.

And, oh yes, brake lights. There should be an internal automotive mechanism in all vehicles which immediately renders inoperative that vehicle upon which the brake lights fail. Coroaders who insist on driving a vehicle with non-functional brake lights should have their licenses immediately suspended. This could be the most dangerous road situation on the I or any other road, bar none. And guess what ... if you hit them, you're probably liable. Maybe that's what they're hoping for. Do yourself and all coroaders a favor and get the non-functional brake light fixed. Probably one of the cheapest safety inventions ever. I have my brakes on; you, behind me, slow down. If you end up behind a vehicle with non-functional brake lights, back way off of that vehicle or change lanes. That's the only safe route. If at all possible, *nicely* tell the coroader that their brake lights are non-functional. If they respond, "I know, I know. They've been that way for weeks," then you can call them any name you please.

BREAKDOWNERS - Everyone will join a jam eventually, not unlike taxes and death. It is a fact of I life. You stop, you wait, you move slowly, you stop again. Time for 1610 AM to find an AR. Horror stories abound ...

"It once took me 50 minutes to go 2 miles on the Garden State!"

Just ask anyone who travels on the I south of Washington, D.C. (the Knot) during the morning or evening. Everyone has a story, and everyone has heard at least two. During the jam frustration is high, tempers flare. There is no good solution to the jam. You must resign yourself to the fact that you will sit. This is a good argument for taking reading material on any trip. It is a good time to reflect on the meaning of life on the I. All the more reason to own some sort of communications.

I, 95

There is one activity some coroaders perform during a jam which is particularly reprehensible... driving in the breakdown lane. It is almost understandable if the coroader is getting off at the next exit one tenth of a mile up the I, but to simply use the breakdown lane for advancement is ridiculous, atrocious, and incredibly dangerous. The reasons need not be explained. Breakdowners universally have small DIQs.

DISLEXITA - Attention and planning ahead have been postulated over and over again. They can not be stressed enough. They will save you and your coroaders untold grief. But, every once in a great while, lack of planning or inattention will strike. One evidence of this is dislexita.

Dislexita occurs when a coroader misses their exit. Ahhh, what to do? The logical, sensible, least dangerous thing to do is continue on up the I and turn around at the next exit[74]. This could be frustrating, especially if the next exit is fifteen miles up the I. Some coroaders simply pull over to a stop, wait for a lull in the traffic, then attempt to back up to a point where they can pull onto the exit ramp. If you look up the word *dangerous* in your Funk and Wagnall's, guess what? Practice this... go to the mall early on a Sunday morning and try backing up in a straight line for about 100 yards. Near impossible. Now imagine performing this act on a highway where the next lane is occupied by vehicles going 65 miles per hour *in the opposite direction!* Now that's dangerous. This action will definitely cause reds all over the I.

Witnessed one Sunday afternoon on the Baltimore - Washington Expressway - one coroader in the left lane (in a

---

[74] Sounds like a good time to practice mappage and AR creation.

I, 95

Mercedes, no less) missed his or her exit, pulled partially onto the median strip in the grass, stopped, then proceeded to back up on the median for about 50 yards. Then, from a standstill, waited for that never-coming lull, and pulled across two lanes of traffic. By the time this had transpired, there were enough reds on this I that the lull was quick in coming. Now, tell me that person is a caring, fellow-man-loving individual. That person has no more notion of driveage that a pygmy. If there were a multi-vehicle pileup behind that Mercedes, that autotator still would have said "Oops" and continued on his or her merry way, completely bypassing the responsibility angle of it all, and in 15 minutes would have completely forgotten the whole incident. Meanwhile, coroaders in the multi-vehicle are sorting out insurance papers, stomping their feet at having been following their quarry too closely. Think.

I, 95

QUESTION: Which side of the road does the fork go on?

DUTY BOOTHS

"Tokens for the I of life."

AB

These little inconveniences are just one of life's certainties, third or fourth in line only to the obvious two or three. So one of an autotator's objectives in I life should be to make them as painless as possible. The first task is to find the perfect lane when approaching the duty booth. This is much like bowling, only the balls are much, much bigger and you are in the finger hole. There is no such thing as the perfect lane because Bowditch's Fifth Law of the I states that no matter what lane you are in, it's the slowest. Even if you decide to switch lanes at the last possible moment, you will just be switching to a lane which will come to an immediate stop. And the length of the lane makes no difference. That guy you have been leapfrogging with for the past twenty miles has been gone for five minutes and has found another partner. It's inevitable. So how do we get through faster?

There is a sign on all roadways that you can spot as you approach the duty booth which states that you should "Reduce Speed." This sign is actually a coded signal from the Department of Transportation which means "Drop Your Logic." More lane-changing takes place in the one quarter mile before the duty booth than in any ten mile stretch of the rest of the I. The coin jockeys vie for position, and don't get in their way. Approaching any duty booth on the Garden State Parkway during the rush

I, 95

time[75] is a nightmare for the token-challenged. There is a wonderful sign on I-95 approaching the Maryland duty booth stating that you should "Reduce Speed NOW." This will give you the last opportunity to find coin of the realm.

Use proper coinage. Make it as simple as possible for the Taker. These people are individuals who are trained in a strenuous classroom environment and have to pass an incredibly arduous final exam. The sole purpose of all this training and testing is to get you through as quickly as possible[76]. Except for the taker whose lane you are in. This person is the one who got a D- on the test, finished 45 out of 45 in the class ranking, but had an uncle in the DOT. So make their job easy. If the duty is for a dollar and twenty-five cents, don't hand the taker two quarters, six dimes, two nickels, and five pennies. This will cause them to quake uncontrollably with the sheer weight of this combination of coin of the realm and make you wait while they count it. Then they will inform you that they don't take pennies. Give them a dollar bill and a quarter, and off you go. If you do not give them as few pieces of coin of the realm as possible, their response will be, "I'm sorry sir [ma'am], we do not accept pennies."

If you know that you'll be going down the same road over and over again, buy tokens. These can be expensed easily and it will certainly add to the enjoyment of the ride when the bell goes off after you miss the bucket for the third time, say the hell with it, and race off. Don't worry, the picture they take of your license plate will probably be fuzzy, anyway.

In most cases, the lanes to the right are the fastest, although Bowditch's Fifth holds here too. So what if that semi is five car lengths long? When he satisfies the taker, he frees up a lot of

---

[75] Rush time on the Garden State Parkway is usually defined as the hours between 4 A.M. and 11 P.M.

[76] Unlike takers at fooders.

space. And you can bet that he has a CORC to beat all CORCs. He's ready, he doesn't want to be there long, he's long enough. Just use common sense when you see a lane with five semis in it.

In the one quarter mile past the duty booth, sensibility breaks down even further. If you thought it was bad in front of the duty booth, just wait to see what's behind it. Courtesy is unknown. More gasoline is expended in this quarter mile than in most of the rest of the I as coroaders attempt to be the first one out of the gate. Most coroaders wear blinders in this section of the I, the Post Booth Brouhaha. Coroaders on the right move left, coroaders on the left move right. There is a five to one ratio of duty booth lanes to travel lanes, so the normal I funnelage is 15 duty booths to the trilane. This will create an unthinkable amount of competition amongst coroaders. Coin jockeys do not resume their normal autotude until well past the duty booth.

If you travel the I for extended periods of time, you will find a peculiar phenomenon occurs relating to duty booths: you will always end up with exact change for all duty booths. No matter what the combination of coin of the realm is required, the exact coinage will always be there for you. This is the Zen of the Exact Change Lane.

I, 95

QUESTION: How many vehicles pass through the Millard Tydings duty booth in Maryland in a day?

TRUCKIN'

"The I was created for them. Automobiles are the aliens."

AB

On a relative scale, these guys use billiard sticks for toothpicks. The Big Guys really know how to drive. By percentage, they are the best autotators out there. If you have never driven one, you can't imagine what it takes to move one of those puppies down the road. Much skill. I was afforded the opportunity to drive one of these tractors in a mall parking lot one Sunday morning. And I thought I was a good autotator. The experience will humble you and force you to reevaluate your driving skills.

The Big Guys have to be better because on many Is we limit them to two lanes, so they have to do what they do not only with larger vehicles, but in a smaller space. We have it easy, we can take any lane we like. We can wander around all we want, buzzing and leapfrogging at will. These guys are trying to deliver goods. That trailer there has on it the dinner you will be cooking tomorrow night. It has on it the juice your children will be drinking this weekend. Are you hungry? Are you thirsty? Let them pass, respect them.

But these rigs pose problems to the average autotator. They are intimidating, mainly. But treated with respect, they will respect us. It doesn't take a lot. The respect we need to give them is primarily room. When you're behind them in the next lane and they want to pull out to pass, flash your lights to let them know it's safe to pull out in front of you. When they pass

I, 95

you, flash your lights to let them know it is all right for them to pull back into the lane. Large objects never forget. They will remember the courtesy.

Many of these rigs have been in some sort of dirty location, especially those units hauling earth moving equipment. These rigs have dirt and rocks on board, and the I, being what it is, has bumps. When these rock carriers hit these bumps, the inevitable happens. This unannounced dislodgment of earth's crust can be particularly unnerving.

Bowditch's Sixth interpreted states that the small pieces of dry land falling from trailers moving at sixty miles per hour will inevitably impact your windshield or expensive obloid headlamp cover. There is no avoiding this. If you move left or right, the exact shape of that small piece of the planet as it hits the pavement will cause it to also move left or right, matching your direction exactly. The trajectory of that small lump of planet is not predictable, again, according to Bowditch's Sixth. As it falls off the moving vehicle, the trajectory is initially low. As it picks up rotational speed, the probability of it impacting the I on a projecting point increases, thus the probability of it being projected straight up into the air (from a relative standpoint) increases dramatically. The height of such a trajectory is dependent upon the speed of the semi and the curvature of the earth at the point of impact, but it will certainly be in direct proportion to the height of your windshield or inconceivably expensive headlamp cover. The solution to this enigma is to slow down or to change lanes. And, of course, this must be planned carefully so as to be done most expediently, with all haste, and without causing reds.

QUESTION: How many gears does the average 18 wheeler have?

I, 95

LANEAGE

"You should be where you need to be."

AB

  A question of semantics: is a country road with one lane going in each direction a one lane or a two lane road? It is obviously a two lane road, so the convention which *should* be used is that the road you are on with three lanes on which you can drive going in the same direction you are autotating has three corresponding lanes on the other side of the divider and is a six lane highway. This means that the divided section of the New Jersey Turnpike is a ten lane road, sometimes twelve. That's a lot of asphalt. That's much too many lanes to have to reference. So we need to refer to each side of the I by itself. A two lane highway refers to your side only, you have two lanes from which to choose. Now ... so what?

  The left lane on any width highway is rarely the fastest (Bowditch's First.) Very few states enforce the "drive right, pass left" philosophy, even though white signage is sometimes posted indicating that it is the law of the land. In Europe, if you are caught doing anything but driving right - passing left[77], you catch a heavy penalty. And they are very strict about that. It is the way things should be. But, here in the US of A, things are different. It is as if the "drive right - pass left" is a recommendation, not a mandate. (This is why there are so many Lefties.) And that is a

---

[77] But don't do it in England.

I, 95

shame, because it does nothing more than to frustrate good autotators.

The left lane should be used for passing and passing only. Lefties notwithstanding, this lane is for everyone breaking the speed limit. The right lane is for pokers, as it should be. The old CB lingo called the right lane the Granny Lane because all the Grandmothers of the world used to drive there. Now these grandmothers have moved left slightly and have sped up to acclimate themselves to their newer, faster Firebirds. The right lane now is used mainly by truckers, Mom 'n' Pops, and sometimes by bedrooms, although bedrooms have also started migrating left since they have an uncanny inability to determine the location of the right side of their vehicles and are afraid of guard rails. There are many places on the I, notably the New Jersey Turnpike, where the right lane is occasionally the fastest lane going.

All other lanes between the rightmost and the leftmost are for all other reasons. Traveling. During I travel, it is easy to fall into a speed groove and feel that anything less than the speed you are maintaining is a snail's pace. But try this sometime: after doing 70 miles per hour for so long, pull over into a middle lane and drop your speed to 60 or 65 miles per hour, or even to the speed limit. It is quite a sensation. You get the eerie feeling that you could push your vehicle faster than you are moving. A little leisurely driveage. So this is the usage intended for these middle lanes. This maneuver is known as "slowage" and is especially easy to do if you are pulling out of a rester or fooder.

No matter what lane you are traversing, there is a phenomenon known as "driving into a cave" or "rolling garage." This is very similar to the Block, but it is always more temporary. Driving into a cave can occur at any time on the I and only requires three automobiles, yours being one of them. The phenomenon occurs when a roader overtakes two coroaders

I, 95

who are traveling *almost* side by side. In pulling behind one coroader, you slip in beside the other, thus eliminating any forward or sideways movement: you are in the cave. The coroader to your left and/or right will usually speed up to trap you in the cave. Driving into a cave can occur in any lane, although if it occurs in the middle lane, there are obviously three coroaders forming the cave. This is very frustrating because the speed differential between the automobiles forming the cave is minimal, and by the time one coroader forming the cave has moved out of the way, another one has moved up to take his or her place. Many coroaders will intentionally go out of their way to create a cave to trap flagrant speeders. This is very satisfying to them to know they have possibly saved the lives of other coroaders. This is a very altruistic scheme, but they must remember that in some portions of particular Is the trapee may be armed. Avoiding a cave requires foresight and planning. Quarter Up.

Guess What? There are multiple standards for lane widths. The standard I lane width is twelve feet. Construction lanes for roads which are being worked on can go as low as ten feet, but it is usually eleven feet. The average automobile width is six feet, nine inches[78], which on a narrow lane allows five feet three inches between automobiles. This seems like a lot, but at 60 miles per hour, this is like passing close to the sun, especially if the occupant of the adjacent lane is a lot larger than you. In the northern reaches of the Garden State Parkway the lanes are narrower than normal (without being in a construction zone), requiring a little more attention to and by coroaders. The people traveling these lanes do not drive cars which are narrower than

---

[78] Outside right rirmir to outside left rirmir, as measured on and averaged between a 1995 Hyundai Elantra (6' 2") and a 1988 Dodge D100 pickup (7' 9").

I, 95

---

normal, but New Jersey needs to allow more cars per road than any other state because there are more cars in the state than the roads will allow[79].

QUESTION: Of what material does the dash consist?

---

[79] I know, I know...the Garden State Parkway is technically not part of the I. Big deal. Try going to New England easily without taking the Garden State Parkway. Tough selection of ARs.

I NICETIES

"Despite the drawbacks, there are I-lights."

AB

    I have seen the top of a lot of Royal Sloans in my travels. After all, on the I everyone has to Sloan eventually[80]. I appreciate the reading material supplied by the Sloan and American Standard[81] companies at the typical rester or fooder, albeit limited. I never knew how many Gallons per Flush (GPF) or Liters per Flush (LPF) were required to whisk away the waste I create. One GPF[82] seems like a lot, but I guess they want to make sure that the stuff I put in the American Standard makes it all the way to wherever it is going. That type of measurement must be very important in those divisions of the ceramics and plumbing industries. If you count how many men, women and children use these facilities each day, that's a major amount of gallons or liters.
    One of the cleverest inventions this century is the Electric (Automatic Flush) Toilet. You just waltz up to the machine and go. Waltz away and the job is done without you having to touch any part of the plumbing except your own. Some sort of infrared

---

    [80] For years I travelers had to put up with pay toilets which, fortunately, have gone the way of the Corvair. Not only did we have to carry coin of the realm for the duty booths, but also for the booths in which we did our duty.

    [81] A company with probably the best slogan in the world... "We've been in the bathroom for over 130 years."

    [82] 3.8 LPF, although Mr. Standard is rounding this figure.

gizmotic technology senses your presence and waits patiently for you to leave. You could stand there all day if you so desired. Really a tribute to modern technology. They don't even have it this good on the space shuttle, although the argument could be made for Permasloans, the Sloan you wear. The only drawback to this great advance in technology it that not everyone is ready for it. Time and time again you can witness people looking foolish while they stand in place and flail at where the flush handle should be. But given all this 20th Century technology, a power outage would surely wreak havoc on Auto-Sloans. Flushless in Fredericksburg.

I was standing in front of one Sloan in Maryland once and noticed that the electronic sensor was flashing. Evidently Auto-Sloans start flashing to indicate to you that it is performing its gizmotic function. User-friendly Urinals. Upon careful inspection, I noticed that it was flashing dot-dot-dot dash-dash-dash dot-dot-dot. I figured that someone was trapped inside, sending Morse to the world to indicate they needed help. This was a good sign that this is not really an infrared sensor, but a real person behind the wall who watched you until you left, then flushed the stall from behind the wall, hopefully with rubber gloves. It seemed that in this instance they were in some sort of trouble. I tried to gain the attention of the attendant in the room, but, unfortunately, I was in a foreign country, unable to communicate in the attendant's tongue. I left the poor wall-bound flusher to fend for himself[83]. If, indeed, there was no person behind the wall, but a machine, then there could be real trouble. Why would a machine attempt to contact the user by

---

[83] *Himself* is used intentionally here because if there was a *herself* behind the wall in the men's rest room, there could be many disturbing legal issues at stake. I am not sure of the state of automation in the lady's room, but I am sure it has to be comparable to the men's room. What happens when you stand up?

signaling SOS through its only contact with the outside world? I had obviously been singled out for some sort of mechano-human interaction.

A clever adjunct to the automatic flush toilet is the automatic water spigot. Again, technology allows us much leisure time in our not having to turn water faucets on or off. I am sure that this invention saves water (and thus, money) and is a boon to the health industry in that no germs are transferred from the spigot to one's hands. These automatic spigots have great entertainment value also. Just watch sometime when some unsuspecting washer attempts to find the spigot without knowing that he (she) should simply put their hands in the sink and allow technology to take over the rest of the process. Inevitably, they walk around the room with their hands in the air in front of them like doctors looking for rubber gloves.

All along the I you have Resters. These are great, use them. The rester, the fooder without the food, the forerunner of the Hojo, actually started as a Scenic Overview, where you could stop, get out of the auto, stroll around and watch over downtown Williamsport, Pennsylvania, or some other city or town with a church steeple and lots of small, cute houses. The facilities at these scenic overviews are sometimes limited[84], but then so are many of the views. Trees grow, views get blocked. Resters are a necessity, to stop and rest. At night, you see them populated with semis. This is good. You know these truckers need a break. Let them rest. Drive through there quietly if you do drive through there at night. Your safety depends on it.

There is a rester in Virginia that has within it a "Pet Rest Area." Think about it. All trip long your pooch is drooling in the back seat of your auto, smiling at the rumble of the road, farting

---

[84] It is beyond the scope of this document to eulogize the iniquities of Plastic Pissers, so aptly named "Johnny on the Spot."

I, 95

to his/her heart's content. Sleep comes easy to many pets. To those who don't travel well, many veterinarians recommend the administration of drugs to your animal so that the trip will be easier on them, and you. This works[85]. So why does the pet need to rest? Obviously the local DOT has a different definition of rest than you and I.

Another nicety is the traffic signs that warn you of impending disaster. (See SIGNAGE.) I believe the first of these was on the New Jersey Turnpike, but California will probably argue this. This New Jersey signage has various configurations which are neoned and limited. They warn you of upcoming congestion, accidents, and fog, but there is no mention of disgruntled postal workers or stupidity. As you approach Baltimore from the north on I-95, there is now signage that warns you of Stadium events at Camden Yards. These Baltimorons are very proud of their stadium, as they should be.

More and more often we now see portable signs (portasignage) which can be programmed, but these have limited sight distance. If there is a four car pile-up in the next lane, you will miss the message because you will not see the portasign while your attention is diverted. As you pass the portasignage you wonder what important piece of information you missed. Could it have been the message that would save you hours achieving Point B-ing. Could it have been the message from your wife reminding you to pick up milk for the children? Is your exit closed? What was it? You feel a sudden urge to pull over, get out and walk back to the portasignage just to see what it said. So you do. You pull over, and trudge back to the sign only to

---

[85] We drugged a cat on a trip from New Jersey to New Hampshire and it was great. The only problem is that you have to get used to the guttural moans which they emanate every now and then as they drape themselves boa-like around your neck. The drugs don't knock them out, they just make them stupid. Just like humans.

I, 95

find "Have a nice day" flashing to the coroaders passing by. The urge to own a shotgun passes through.

I, 95

QUESTION: How much toilet paper does the Maryland House go through in one day?

FOODAGE

"There are no drive-thrus on the I."

AB

Where to Find Food

The Hojo days are over. Howard Johnson, the Fooder Pioneer, pulled out of the now historic Orange Roof fooder business during the gas crunch and decided motels were the thing. The only conclusion is that if you can't drive, at least you have to sleep. Now the fooders are Bob's Big Boys, Roy Roger's, and some place called Sbarro's. That is not pronounceable. TCBY is coming on strong and you don't have to know how to pronounce it. If you want a burger or a roast beef sandwich or chicken and fries or a high-fat yogurt ice-cream-looking cone, you can get what you want. It's typical "fast" food because it was prepared yesterday and it tastes like it, although you should be leery of two-day-old yogurt. The only option is to stop there during the rush time and shove and push your way through the crowds to get at the food as soon as it is put under the spot heaters, although spot heaters are not recommended for yogurt. That's the only way you know it is "fresh." Otherwise, you will get the burger/chicken/pizza from yesterday which will truly test your teeth. All these fooders are the same. But be nice...

The person serving these delights is another human being there to serve the public. They should be treated with all the

I, 95

respect due them. This Taker will appreciate correct change and will make your life (and the lives of the people behind you) miserable if you hand them a twenty for a soda. But, take heart! In a few years you will have to offer up a twenty for a soda. Takers are human beings, too. Sometimes it is hard to believe, but it is true. If you can catch one at the start of a shift, they can be pretty pleasant. However, after careful study, it has been proven that takers actually start all their shifts in the middle, so that there is no "start" of the shift.

On one trip along the Massachusetts Turnpike a group of 5 of us ex-college know-it-alls stopped at the Hojo after the I-84 entrance. It was early Saturday morning and we had been visiting an all-girl college in western Massachusetts. We were high as kites and hungry for that wonderful Hojo breakfast. The parking lot was stuffed with New York and New Jersey campers of all kinds heading for the hills (on the Eastbound side?) of New England. Inside you could hear a pinhead drop, even though the place was absolutely packed. It was so subdued we thought someone had had too many scrambled eggs. We found a table and waited. Eventually our waitress showed up. She was haggard. It was obvious she had been dealing with people who had been on the road for hours and wanted to be pampered, and then not pay for it. You could tell from her look that the tips had been slim, if at all. And she had bright orange hair. When it came to me to order, I popped the obvious question: "Did you get your job here because you have an Orange Roof, too?"

Maryland has two above standard places to stop, the Maryland House (southern) and the Chesapeake House (northern). Both of these are in the median, so you have to exit left and aggravate everyone going 75 in the left lane. They are quite different in architecture and the Chesapeake House has a "Farmer's Market" open all year long, although it seems like nothing more than a glorified gift shop. Both have Travel

I, 95

Centers which are full of an unimaginable amount of tourist information, including the Decoy Hall of Fame and the Ordnance Museum. There is always a place to park if you are willing to walk, and you know you need to get some sort of exercise. The Maryland House is on top of a hill, so slowing down on arrival and speeding up on exit is a breeze. The Chesapeake House is also on top of a hill, but the northbound egress back onto the I is up the next hill. Both Houses have three types of gas: Exxon, Texaco and Roy Rogers.

The one Delaware fooder[86] is clean, and far less crowded than average. It is simple to park near the door, especially northbound. But be careful once inside. You are blitzed with places to eat (including Sbarro's) and things to do, but beware: the exits from the building are labeled NORTH and SOUTH, so you have to remember where you are going. The oddest part of this is that these exits are on the East and West sides of the building. I have witnessed many people walking around the building looking for their significant others and wondering which car they were driving. Their only hope is that some family member will recognize them and yell something. If they are traveling alone it means they will have to circle the building until two a.m. when the parking lot is a lot less full and their senses return.

Even if the parking lot of any fooder is empty, there is an unpleasant practice performed by certain ethical groups that is truly aggravating: parking in front of the restaurant, right by the door. This is not only disrespectful, but dangerous. There are very few pedestrian right-of-ways at fooders, at least none that

---

[86] Delaware, being the size it is, only has room for one fooder. If there were more than one, the exit from the first would be the entrance to the second.

anyone respects, and these pedestrians become fair game areas. The people who park there are probably,

1. Ignorant

2. Fat

3. Lazy

4. Ethically challenged.

    If it's time to stop at a fooder, park as far away from the front door as possible, the walk will do you good. If you sit for hours, your arse will undoubtedly be dunched and it will need exercise. Aside from a health spa, which you will not find at a fooder, you can only do deep knee bends and stretching exercises when you stop. Do them. The designers of these fooders and resters should put the restaurants 1/4 mile from the parking lot to force us all to walk. People with handicaps need the exercise as much as the rest of us, with only limited exceptions.
    After leaving the fooder or rester, you have to repack. Prior to the stop, you were with a group of coroaders whom you had psychoautolyzed, so you knew everything about their autotude, including what idiotic moves they were likely to make. Now, after that drain and fill, it's time to make new friends, to readjust to the new group you are about to join. You have to be attentive, because now you have to psychoautolyze this new pack to figure out who you can trust, who to watch out for, who to avoid at all costs, and who would make a good partner for leapfrog. Typically, three miles is the average distance requirement for this autotude readjustment. And remember, when starting to repack, pulling out of the fooder must be done

with bravery and skill. Do not leave the fooder at any speed less than the speed limit. Many fooders are now in the median strip which means that, when you leave them, you are entering the left lane. Most people in the left lane are attempting to go excessively fast, so you have to merge gracefully. And they are coming at you from your blind spot. Repack as quickly and as carefully as possible.

Stopping at a fooder or rester is highly recommended when confronted with a block. Lengthy blocks can get frustrating and it will take time to get through them. Stop, rest, then repack. The block will be far down the road, merrily ticking people off, while you have readjusted your autotude and settled back down to business. Even if you do not buy food, but have had the foresight to pack your own food in a cooler in the trunk, it is a good idea to stop and stretch.

Simply because you are on the I does not mean that you have to eat where there are fooders. If you know you are going to be on the I for some time, it may be worthwhile to pack your own. This means having the space for a cooler in which you can deposit ice, liquid, and solid refreshment. Just use a little common sense in what you pack. If you are going to stop and eat (highly recommended), then you can pack anything. But if you are going to get stop, get some food, then get back on the I, then you must think about what will drop in your lap as you are driving. Things like mustard will stain, and it is very doubtful that you will have club soda available. If you have planned far enough ahead to have club soda available, then you have the wrong job.

I, 95

The following is a small list of yeas and nays:

Recommended:

    Dry sandwiches

    Crackers

    "Bite-sized" food

Not recommended:

    Hot dogs with mustard and relish

    Spaghettios

    "Foot-long" subs

Where Not to Find Food

Anywhere on the New Jersey Turnpike, especially the Northern half.

There is one exception and that is the 1995 renovated Molly Pitcher rester southbound. It's clean because it's new, but by the time you read this, that will have changed. And it is not very well planned. It is a long walk to the American Standard.

I, 95

Do not eat anywhere on the Garden State Parkway, especially the Northern half. There are McDonald's along the Northern section of the Garden State Parkway, but these are not well maintained. There seems to be a definite attitude surrounding these places. Imagine Ronald with a knife. Kind of scary.

Of course, if you have totally custom-tailored your auto for the I, you have an ice box. This solves all the normal fooder problems because you can now eat when and where you like. Pack it with whatever you want, stop when and where you want, chow down. I traveled throughout Arizona in a van which also served as my home. Stopping to eat was always a pleasure because Arizona is a beautiful state and there is always something old to enjoy.

Spicy food is out. Eat plain. You don't want to ruin your upholstery and those little pine trees are really tacky.

New Jersey Turnpike Fooders

These fooders are named after famous people who are either from, oddly enough, New Jersey, had lived there most of their lives, or had performed some sort of activity there, like die. Some of these are relatively well-known, others are more obscure. In this rather strange tribute to these people, New Jersey has committed itself to maintaining these fooders in the same standards of excellence to which these luminaries dedicated their lives. They would be proud.

<u>Vince Lombardi</u> – This is indeed interesting… Vincent Thomas Lombardi was born on June 11, 1913, in Brooklyn,

I, 95

N.Y. So what does he have to do with New Jersey? Nothing, until 1939. His first non-scholastic playing experience was with the Wilmington (DE) Clippers in 1937. In 1939 he took a teaching and coaching job at St. Cecilia High School in Englewood, N.J. This was his only connection to New Jersey. So they honored him with a fooder.

    James Fennimore Cooper - The real name of this fooder is J. Fennimore Cooper because if it was called the James F. Cooper area, no one would know who it was. James Fennimore Cooper was born in Burlington, New Jersey on September 15th, 1789. Burlington, New Jersey in 1789 must have been a days ride from the nearest city. Famous for *The Last of the Mohicans* (1826), *The Deerslayer* (1841), and other novels of woodsy nature, James Fennimore Cooper would be shocked and dismayed with Burlington today. This man was obviously ahead of his time for his novel *The Pathfinder* (1840) was used to name a popular vehicle on the I, and another novel, *The Redskins* (1846) was used by Washington to name their team.

    Grover Cleveland - Born in Caldwell, New Jersey on March 18th, 1837, Grover Cleveland's claim to fame is that he was the only president to serve two non-consecutive terms; he was the 22nd and 24th President. Today, when we think of Grover, most people would respond with references to Sesame Street. No wonder, much of Cleveland's support came from the "Mugwumps", possibly a Sesame Street creation.

    Molly Pitcher - Born Mary Ludwig Hayes in Trenton, New Jersey on August 20th, 1795, Molly (as her friends called her) Pitcher grew up and married Mr. McCauley and became Mary

Ludwig Hayes McCauley. The Molly Pitcher nickname came during the Revolutionary War when she carried pitchers of water to the American troops. Must have carried a lot of water.

Joyce Kilmer - Born in New Brunswick, New Jersey in 1886, Joyce's only claim to fame is "Trees", probably New Jersey trees. We must be thankful, though, that our parents were not like Joyce's parents in their unconventional child naming: Joyce's sister was named Fred. Joyce's *real* first name was Alfred.

John Fenwick - This fooder personality is a strange one. Fenwick was born in England in 1674 and brought up a Quaker. Through some strange land-sharing scheme, Jack (as his friends called him) was assigned land originally assigned to Lord Berkley by Edward Byllynge. In 1675, John founded Salem, the first permanent English settlement. Due to some conflict with a Sir Edmund Andros, John was thrown in the clinker, thus creating a heritage shared by many New Jersey Land Barons, including Jimmy Hoffa[87]. The dispute with Sir Edmund was settled when John gave up all his rights to the land to William Penn (truly a name-dropper this Jack) for 150,000 acres of land somewhere else. Probably the Pine Barrens.

Richard Stockton - Born in Princeton, New Jersey in 1730, Dick (to his friends) became a lawyer. He tried to reconcile the conflict between England and the Colonies, historically to no

---

[87] Although Mr. Hoffa was actually not from New Jersey. He was born in Brazil, Indiana. He just resides in New Jersey.

I, 95

avail. In 1776 he was elected to the Continental Congress. Captured by the British at some point, he was treated harshly, released, and died in 1781 of that harsh treatment. Probably some sort of tea allergy.

<u>Alexander Hamilton</u> - Another politician, known primarily for passing his Ten Dollar Bill. Born in Nevis, West Indies, Alex was the illegitimate son of James Hamilton and Rachel Fawcett Laurien, daughter of a rich rancher, proving beyond the shadow of a doubt that *anyone* of dubious moral character can become Secretary of the Treasury. Alex, as his friends knew him, became a New York lawyer at that incredibly short period in time when there were not that many lawyers in New York. Possibly he was following in the footsteps of Dick Stockton. His only tie to New Jersey is his death in Weehawken Heights at the hands (gun) of Aaron Burr.

<u>Woodrow Wilson</u> - Despite having his face on a dime, a $100,000 bill and a bridge between Maryland and Virginia, Tom (to his buddies) is actually named Thomas Wilson. The 28th president is primarily known for the fooder created in his honor. Born in Staunton, Virginia in 1856 he wandered around the Blue Ridge Mountains for some time before ending up at Princeton University. He graduated there in 1879 and later (1902) became president of that University. He also served as Governor of New Jersey before becoming president. By the way, there are no $100,000 bills in circulation and the bridge is in a terrible state of disrepair. His dimes are in good condition, though.

Thomas Edison - Probably the most famous New Jersey non-native, Tom's accomplishments are quite well known. Born in Milan, Ohio in 1847, he immediately gave up his right to be a native of Ohio. But no one held this against him. He maintained a workshop in West Orange, New Jersey, so they erected a memorial in Menlo Park, New Jersey. Makes perfect sense. His primary contribution to life, of course, is the cartoon idea balloon.

I, 95

SPECIAL FOODER BONUS!! TWO QUESTIONS!!

QUESTION: What was the name of Roy Roger's dog?

QUESTION: Where was the first I HOJO?

I, 95

PLACE NAMES

"No matter what you call it, there's no place like home." [88]

AB

Along The Mid-Atlantic there are place names on green signage that catch the autotator's eye. Some are almost comical, all are unique.

Port Deposit, Maryland[89]

This is a rather strange name. It implies some sort of tax collection for boats going up the river to .... somewhere up the river. Port Deposit is the smallest town in the United States that has no room to grow. It is bounded by the Susquehanna River and walls of granite. No where to go but up.

Rising Sun, Maryland

A town with this name can only be on the East Coast. There must be a town in California or Oregon or Washington called, yes, Setting Sun.

---

[88] With apologies to Dorothy.

[89] Maryland, by the way, has one of the nicest state flags in the country.

I, 95

Millard Tydings Bridge

Running across the I-95 in Maryland is a bridge crossing the Susquehanna River known as the Millard Tydings Bridge[90]. This bridge is very high off of the river and the view is worth slowing down for, but be careful. Dangerous X-winds[91] exist in this area.

Millard Tydings was not a very popular personality.

There are probably not many people besides descendants who can name his accomplishments. Born in Havre de Grace, Maryland (just down the I from the bridge) in 1890, Milly (as his friends called him, much to the chagrin of his sister Millie, who always answered the phone for him) was a member of the Maryland legislature and later the U.S. House of Representatives. He was opposed to many of the policies of FDR, which did not help his popularity. The kicker, though, was that he headed the Senate Sub-committee appointed to investigate Senator McCarthy. Real popular job.

The Mixing Bowl - Southbound

Arguably one of the worst traffic areas in the western world, this is the rhubarb of the I. Ask anyone who drives there. It has been nicknamed the Mixing Bowl, but it should be called the Knot, because you're knot going to get through there easily. The Mixing Bowl is not for the neophyte. Just south of Washington, D.C., it comprises I-95 from the east, I-395 from the north, I-495 from the west, and who knows what roads from the local area. Four lane Is constricting down to two for an exit/entrance to the I-95 south create havoc, a freeway-for-all. Then, after that

---

[90] You can see Port Deposit from here.
[91] Alien flatulence.

gets straightened out, there's the Eternal Construction Company doing business creating HOV lanes. There are so many HOV lanes that you cannot travel this portion of the road unless you have six people in your Yugo with you. This portion of I-95 south of the Washington Beltway will never be the way it should be, there will always be construction. By the time the current project is finished, it will be outdated and will need revamping, reramping and new barriers put up. And to have two HOV lanes narrow down to zero is absurd. This road was designed by the Congress of the United States. Most of the coroaders here are government workers, whose purpose in life is to watch their respective department's progress and see how well it has been botched.

Mullica Hill, New Jersey

The name of this southern New Jersey town rolls off of the tongue. Easy to say, the initial "Mu" sound means you can start saying this word even before you open your mouth. Mullica Hill is not famous for anything, although the town fathers and mothers would probably argue this. Mullica Hill evokes visions of Apple Festivals sometime during the harvest. There must be Tomato and Pumpkin Festivals to enjoy here at some points during the year.

I, 95

Rancocas Woods, New Jersey

    This name evokes visions of Sherwood Forrest and Robin Hood. Possibly, though, it was the inspiration for the Beatles song *Rocky Raccoon*. Rancocas Woods has as many claims to fame as Mullica Hill.

Rio Grande, New Jersey

    Really? This South-of-the-New York-Border town is in southern New Jersey, not really near an I, but spotted on the side of a semi on the I, so it still counts. The Spanish-speaking population is probably very laid back, and there must be a plethora of cowboy hats and pickup trucks.

QUESTION: Is there a "good" time to pass inconsequentially through The Mixing Bowl?

MAPPAGE

"I'm not lost. I know exactly where I am."

AB

All these wonderful place names and locations would be near impossible to find if it were not for maps. Transversing the I can be a "no-brainer." If you know that Point B-ing is just off the I in Portland, Maine, you can drive that far and get off the I when you see green signage indicating "Portland." Your only fear should be that you have driven clear to Oregon. All you have to do is stop at the necessary fooders and resters to arrive there safely. ARs are not necessary unless jams are outrageous. But, what about the unplanned side trip? Can you get off the I, side trip, specify an AR, and get back on the I gracefully?

Mappage is simply the ability to read and interpret a map, or a relatively complete collection of maps. It is nothing more than that. You do not have to be a direct descendant of Amerigo Vespucci or Lewis or Clark[92], you simply have to practice the ability to know where you are, where you want to go, and in which direction to proceed. Sextants are not necessary; however, knowing that the sun rises in the east and sets in the west is a requirement[93]. Take time out prior to your I journey to pull out

---

[92] Who all did what they did without mappage.

[93] Since there are relatively few trees on the immediate I (the paved portion), it is not considered important to know upon which side of the tree the moss grows.

I, 95

the DeLorme, find Point A, find Point B, and find all the routes in between.

One key is recognizing the intermediate points between A and B which could be important. Then, while on the I, recognizing signage which could lead to these important points. There are *at least* four different ways to get from Hartford, Connecticut to Newark, New Jersey. Which one is the best? That depends upon quite a bit of information - the time of the year, the time of the day, and the Jupiter Effect. Create AR creativity. This key is knowing the ARs between A and B and the only way to do this is with decent mappage.

Another key is to visualize the route and the intermediate points on the way to Point B-ing. The only way to do this is to peruse the DeLorme ahead of time. Plan ahead. The map of Connecticut printed in 1965 is probably about seventy percent accurate in 1995. The Federal government has proven time and time again that an old road is no good. Move it, change it, make it wider, but during construction, make it narrower. Then let the map makers catch up to what they are supposed to do. There are no announcements to the map makers which state, "Hey, we're going to move I-95 in North Carolina 5 miles west." The map makers have to keep their eyes and ears open[94]. Examples of incorrect or out of date mappage-caused problems are common:

In Richmond, Virginia the roads are changing so often that highways listed on maps printed in 1990 are now continued farther, so that if you expect to get off the I, you won't, because you don't have to , and you continue on past the dotted line on the map to a new, unknown location.

Years ago there was an exit (Exit 50) off of the Baltimore Beltway years back labeled "Future." People would get real

---

[94] So how do they do this? Are there special road crews that just travel the Is and note the changes?

I, 95

excited about getting off and seeing what the future was like. But to their tremendous disappointment, the next exit was 51 (or 49 depending on one's direction of travel) and suddenly they realized that there was no future.

How do you keep current? Look for the newest DeLorme. If you belong to a road service such as AAA or AA or whatever it is, take advantage of the map services they offer. They are usually the most current[95]. But still check the date on the map when you receive it, you may be able to do better.

Used to be that maps were free[96] until some enterprising SOB[97] realized that he could make a killing if they sold the maps instead of giving them away. No more lining the canary cage with downtown Baltimore. Now you have to fork over $2.95 every two years for every map just to keep abreast[98]. Well, it is worth it. You drive, you ought to know where you are going. For about 12 bucks you can get the large, detailed version and find every I between Bangor, Maine and San Diego, California. A current map is worth its weight in asphalt.

Again, take advantage of any mappage services if you belong to any of the travel services. The travel service mappage is not free[99], but they explain in linear detail straight-ahead Point B-ing and continue the fallacy that someone else knows your agenda better than you do. These services provide the service that you cannot "afford" to perform. Bull. You should be your own driveage service. You know how to do it, you just don't want to spend the time. So you do have the time; get up from in

---

[95] Remember, they have their road crews out looking.
[96] Sounds like the lyrics to an old song by Bob Dylan.
[97] Sounds like the lyrics to an old song by Guns 'n' Roses.
[98] Some states supply maps free of charge. Stop in at the Maryland House and visit the Travelers Center. It's a model for what they should all look like and how they should perform.
[99] Well, you paid for the service, didn't you?

I, 95

front of the TV Guide and break out the DeLorme. You can do it. It's easy once you apply yourself. It becomes a wonderful, scenic challenge planning ARs through places with names like Forks of Buffalo, Virginia and Gualala, California. If you're not in much of a hurry, stop in Havre de Grace, Maryland and see the Decoy Museum. No AAA mappage is going to show that unless you check the "Incredibly Scenic Route" box on the mappage request form for the trip between Miami, Florida and Portland, Maine. That's too much mappage for the service to provide. The postage alone would put them out of business.

There is such a thing as bad mappage. It is usually easy to spot. Be leery if:

The map of Indiana you are perusing was printed in Taiwan.

Place names look like "Wsahingtin, C.D."

Any cemeteries are listed in the "Points of Interest" section.

Locations of High Schools are indicated with daggers.

North Dakota and South Dakota are interchanged.

There are many more subtle indications of bad mappage, but the examples here serve to point out the more glaring errors which could occur there.

Folding a map back to its original configuration has been one of the reasons for the state of the economy for years, for reasons totally outside the realm of this book. All map makers create maps for a state which make the state much look larger than it actually is. You can travel for seven inches and be in the next state. Glancing at the map to find your exact location gives one a great sense of accomplishment and pride - "I am here!" But now you have to put the map back in the map box or pocket, and that means folding it. An Independent University study of map boxes and door pockets, found that only seven percent of the maps were folded correctly, and these usually in automobiles with anal-retentive owners. There is a definite art to folding that sixteen page map of Rhode Island. Some colleges offer courses to aid you in this.

With the advances in technology coming as fast as they are, it is amazing how we can find the time to master something before it is out of date. Most people now can fold a map with eighty percent accuracy. And now maps are becoming obsolete. You can purchase software for your home computer which will plan your route for you and print you a map. Sort of like AAA in a box. There is also the future in Global Positioning Systems (GPS) which will utilize satellites to tell you where you are and what road you should be on to get to where you want to go. Some people may find this rather intrusive. Big Brother is not only watching you, he is telling you where to go. Can you imagine the scandal if everyone on the I ended up at the same place? Talk about your jams!!

I, 95

QUESTION: Who was responsible for the first map of the United States?

ODDITIES

"What makes I life interesting is out of the ordinary,"

AB

We all need access to things which will make us laugh or think. Signs for the following items have appeared mystically on the side of various roads and would make an autotator laugh or think. Some of these can be classified as "Points of Interest" while others are just plain odd.

The Decoy Museum - Approaching Havre de Grace, Maryland (I 95 Exit 89) there is Informational signage advertising the Decoy Museum. One would assume that these are duck decoys, primarily because of the proximity of Havre de Grace and the Museum to the water of the upper regions of the Chesapeake, although that could be wrong. It is a must to stop there to find out if these decoys are samples of works, or if this is the decoy Hall of Fame[100]. One would then expect to see battle-scarred veterans of the Potomac, their little wooden bodies filled with buckshot from errant sightings of the real

---

[100] But make it quick, they're only open from 11 A.M. to 4 P.M.

I, 95

feathered item. If not a duck decoy museum, then what? Cardboard cutouts of life-sized elephants on the savanna?

Ft. McHenry Tunnel - The main I-95 tunnel under the Inner Harbor in Baltimore has manhole[101] covers in it. Now, where do these go? Is there something under the tunnel? Must be where the trolls live. They are more likely to be plugs disguised as manhole covers designed to keep the water out. If you are ever in the tunnel and see water coming out any of these manhole covers, the fifty mile per hour speed limit should be ignored, quickly.

Rumble Strips - Approaching the Delaware duty booth from the north you run across (literally) a real eye-opener called rumblestrips[102]. These lateral cuts in the road really do serve a purpose: to wake you up to the fact that in not so many feet there is a definite stopping point in the road, the feared duty booth. Rumblestrips have been observed in locations other than duty booth approaches. Many portions of I 95 now have rumblestrips along the entire edge to keep you out of the weeds. Entrances to sharp curves are also candidates for rumblestrips.

The Ordnance Museum - Just south of the Havre de Grace Decoy museum is another gem in Maryland's crown, the Aberdeen Ordnance Museum. Sponsorships are available to ex-

---

[101] I am deferring to the historic usage of the word and refraining from calling these large, heavy disks "personhole" covers.
[102] Yes, they do exist in other parts of the I world, but this location is the most prominent on the Mid-Atlantic routes.

marines and members of the NRA. This would be a real neat place to take the wife and other family members while on vacation. Go visit bullets which fought in various wars. Some of these should be famous. But be aware that this is not the Bullet Hall of Fame, it is the Ordnance Museum. Which implies that this ordnance is obsolete. Wouldn't it be nice if all ordnance was obsolete? Talk to your coroaders about this. But stop at the museum first. It is open Armed Forces Day, Independence Day, Memorial Day, and Veterans Day (and most normal days) from 12 noon to 4:45 P.M. It is closed Mondays[103].

The New Jersey State Police Museum - During a lull in a jam in New Jersey, a radio spot on 1610 AM advertised the State Trooper Hall of Fame. The radio spot droned on to state that there is an Audio-Visual display showing the highlights of the Lindbergh kidnapping. This is great. The state troopers probably do not get the glory that, say, fighter pilots or New York City detectives receive, so a museum is a good idea. Give them something to shoot for. The museum is in West Trenton.

The Masters, Mates and Pilots Association Training Center - Approaching Baltimore from the south on I-295 (Baltimore - Washington Expressway) there is a sign advertising the training center for the Masters, Mates and Pilots Association. It is a part of some Union of sorts, not the Union of the states, but of the International Brotherhood of People on Water. They pilot boats with a large "T" on the stern to let overtaking vessels know that there is a rookie at the helm.

---

[103] What happens if Armed Forces Day, Independence Day, Memorial Day, or Veterans Day fall on a Monday?

I, 95

The Shrine of Our Lady of the Highway - The Oblates of Saint Francis de Sales maintain the Shrine of Our Lady of the Highways in Childs, Maryland, a landmark of sorts. There is a statue erected there ("The Stone Lady") in memory of three people who died in an accident on that spot on the I in 1968. The unusual shrubbery was planted in 1979 by Father John Conmy and a group of 4-H Club members. The "V J" stands for Vive Jesus. This odd creation of stone and ornamental planting serves as a reminder for us all to drive defensively. Let's do it.

The Fire Museum of Maryland - Outside of Baltimore (Exit 26 off of the Beltway) is this Museum dedicated to fighting fires. There is a collection of fire-fighting apparati dating back to 1822. Memberships are available[104]. All one has to do is prove they can start and stop a fire in a small apartment building. The Museum is equipped with the most statest-of-the-art fire extinguishing system available.

The Lacrosse Hall of Fame - Again, Baltimore has outshone many other Right Coast cities in their propensity for Museums and Halls of Fame. This one claims to capture the ambiance of the three hundred and fifty year history of Lacrosse with a fifty foot timeline of the games greatest moments, both of them. If you have never seen a Lacrosse game, take a few moments to watch one. It will make Ice Hockey look tame.

---

[104] Arsonists need not apply.

I, 95

QUESTION: If someone had to cover the rumblestrip, what would they use?

I, 95

1610 AM

"The only psychic channel worth listening to on the I."

AB

AM radio died ages ago, although I am sure any proponent of this position would hear many arguments to the contrary from owners of AM radio stations. Okay, apology proffered. But on the I, the AU cassette tape deck is the only way to travel ... except in a potential jam.

Many states now support AM radio stations broadcasting news and information about the current status of that particular section of the I you are transversing. This is known as the Traveler's Advisory Radio, or TAR. In late 1995 or early 1996, something called the I-95 Corridor Coalition was formed to monitor and dispense information about road conditions on the I. This Coalition covers from Maine to Virginia[105]. This AM station is usually 1610 AM. Unfortunately, they do not *always* tell you any alternate routes, only that you are in a traffic situation which has come to a complete stop. In idle moments, some of these 1610 stations even give you local events so that if you want to stop and take in a little local scenery, they make it easy to pick out something to do, all within easy reach of the I.

---

[105] There is something about jams in the Carolinas, Georgia and Florida that is not worth reporting. Once you get past The Knot it is clear sailing.

I, 95

The New Jersey Turnpike and Maryland are great for this. They are accurate and give good reports. Delaware is not quite as good. In a state-long jam in Delaware, the 1610 contained only static. On another trip with clear roads, the 1610 proclaimed that the road was clear with no jams. Thanks a great deal.

Unfortunately, the 1610 nicety is not quite universal. The Washington, D.C. Beltway (part of which is actually I-95) uses 1290 AM. Not that this is a terrible travesty on commonality, but it is an inconvenience. And 1290 on the Washington Beltway must be incredibly busy. Never a dull moment on that I. The announcers on that TAR are retired auctioneers.

The 1610 is great, whatever band it is on, except, of course, in Delaware. If you enter a state or change Is and see a sign informing you to check the AM band for local I traffic conditions, it is worth the few minutes it takes to listen to the report. Who knows, you may find that the Saint Aloycious Pancake Festival is in full swing and worth the stopover.

QUESTION: Between what two cities did Marconi send the first transatlantic wireless transmission?

CONSTRUCTION

"It must be someone's job to make things better."

AB

Construction is an absolute necessity. Road surfaces wear down, bridges deteriorate[106]. So inevitably, you and all your coroaders will run up against some sort of construction. It does seem amazing, though, that roads are made of cement or asphalt and all the typical roader has to challenge that with is rubber. Just imagine how many rubber tires must have passed over that section of cement or asphalt to damage it. So what gives? The asphalt? In the north, there is the Great Pothole Conspiracy, formed when water makes its inevitable way through the crevices in the construction processes and then freezes, forcing that material up, only to be beaten about by the incredibly strong rubber of your tires, finally forming the hole which will wear minute particles off of your tires.

Then the construction crews move in with their New Jersey Barriers, those wonderful too-close-to-my-car cement monoliths. And you are forced to use attention to the "Traffic Fines Doubled in Construction Zones" signs and realize that the lane you are in has narrowed to eleven or ten feet. Okay, what's the definition of a construction zone? Do you ever see a "Start of Construction Zone" sign? Well, you do, but it is usually well past

---

[106] Pleasant thought, huh? Just when will it be determined that the bridge you are on is impassable?

I, 95

the start of the construction zone and it doesn't say "Start of Construction Zone." It will say something like "One lane open - 12 feet." You see an "End Zone" sign well past the end of the construction zone. So where do the MCs hang out? At the start, of course.

Most jams encountered along the I are not the result of the overzealous coroader or the occasional fender-bender, but by the ever-present eternal construction zone. Many of these construction zones are temporary[107], such as pothole filling, and some are the more permanent "please do it right this time" bridge repairs, but one thing they all have in common is that they displace at least one lane of traffic. If we assume that 1) an automobile is traveling at sixty miles per hour, 2) every automobile is fifteen feet long, and 3) every automobile is maintaining seventy-three feet between itself and the automobile in front of it, then an automobile passes any spot on the I once every second. For a trilane, then three automobiles per second pass a given spot[108]. If the *X*DOT[109] decides that now is the time to repair that pesky pothole, they will claim one of those lanes in the name of the DOT and the Eternal Construction Company will set up shop. Now we have three automobiles per second merging into two lanes or less. They will not fit as comfortably as we would like to think. Well, they would if we all cooperated.

---

[107] The term "temporary" takes on a different relative meaning when applied to construction zones. The shortest recorded time period for a construction zone was August 22, 1967 in Atlanta, Georgia when a construction zone was set up to fill in potholes. The temperature at 9 a.m. reached 95 degrees and it was determined to be too hot to work. The construction zone was in place for twenty-two minutes. No potholes were filled.

[108] Brilliant, huh?

[109] *X* is any state initials.

I, 95

At any construction zone, autotators may or may not get plenty of warning that the construction zone is pending[110], and which, if any, lane will no longer exist. Yet there seems to be a game afoot which goes something like this: any autotator who can come as close to the cones or barrels without touching them will be dubbed King (or Queen) of the Closed Lane. There are no rules to this game, and the playing field may even include the breakdown lane, if necessary. So we narrow the I to two lanes from three, and if we include the breakdown lane, to two lanes from four. This will obviously cause consternation amongst coroaders who are trying to maintain some semblance of flow.

By the time we reach the construction zone, we are no longer speeding along at sixty miles per hour because we are now too concerned with position, trying to cut each other off in the process of determining which lane is the best[111]. Wouldn't it be a blessing if everyone approaching a lane-closing construction zone merged at the first sign of lane closure? Traffic may even pass through the construction zone at the recommended speed limit. And that speed limit has been determined to be optimal just in case one of the members of the crew strays into the remaining open lanes.

The personnel at the construction site (construction personnel) are always milling about. These are members of the Professional Millers Association (PMA)[112]. This union was started by Jimmy Hoffa before his interment in that permanent construction zone in the Meadowlands. The Miller's Union. I wonder what the pay scale is?

---

[110] This depends *entirely* upon the Jupiter Effect.
[111] A modified Bowditch's Fourth applies here.
[112] Not to be confused with the Professional Millers Society (PMS) which is found at bakeries throughout the country.

133

I, 95

And those lovely cones, or barrels, the one you covet and desire just in case the need should arise for use in your driveway or garage. They have those wonderfully brilliant fluorescent orange colors and reflective stripes. And there are so many of them. The CBAU (Cone and Barrel Alignment Union) is hard at work perfecting the straightest line ever or the most graceful curve heading for the breakdown lane. For years it has been baffling as to where these cones and barrels were stored. Then after driving and researching, the answer was discovered. They are stored right where they are. There are so many construction projects forever evolving on the I that the need for these cones and barrels is ever-constant. They are stored right where they sit. When their function at that location is complete, they simply move down the I to the next, new construction site. All that is required is the cone/barrel transport truck. The person who has the responsibility of driving the truck and moving these cones or barrels from one location to the next has a full time job. They are permanent members of the CBAU, Traffic Division. Definitely not a member of the Miller's Union.

QUESTION: What is the average cost to construct one mile of I?

EXERCISE

"No one gains weight on the I."

AB

It is very important to maintain sanity and physical well-being while on the I. Sanity on the I, of course, is a near impossibility, simply because of the demanding strains put on an autotator by coroaders, Bubbles, Construction Zones, and the Jupiter Effect. Seasoned I drivers usually have a screw loose somewhere. But physical I well-being is achievable.

The sitting position does not lend itself well to any serious form of exercise, unless your throne happens to be a vibrating exercise bike. Then adjusting the rirmirs becomes a tiresome full-time job. But there are a few exercises which, although not an entire regimen, will aid in the circulation of blood and other fluids necessary to attain Point B-ing without having to stop by to visit that Irish friend, O'Besity. These exercises are by no means complete, but they will help you maintain that incredible muscle tone so laboriously worked for while not on the I.

HANDS - Exercising both hands at once is definitely not recommended while on the I. That errant pothole could ruin your whole day. One of the easiest exercises to do (with one hand) is the squeeze ball. This could be nothing more than a strong rubber balloon filled with sand. Simply squeeze to your heart's content to exercise the muscles. Another unit is the spring-shaped exerciser. Although good, it is harder to store than the squeeze ball. Another hand exercise is using those

I, 95

clinky Chinese balls. Large metal ball-bearings will do, but the enameled ones that come in that tacky obviously-made-in-China covered box and make some sort of mentally soothing wind chime noise are great for impressing no one at all. But they work. Just be careful in near jams. If you have to drop them in a hurry, you could be distracted from driveage by the sudden pain in your leg, lap or foot.

ARMS - Exercising the arms is a little tougher because there is just no room to do pushups in the front seat. One thing you can do is stretch them out fully and flex them. Just make sure you ease your grip on the steerage unit before attempting this. No need to bother the coroaders to your left or right with your exercise routine. You can also grab the crashboard and push up and down. Or put your hands flat on the roof and push. For maximum effect, it is recommended that the sun roof be closed.

STOMACH - About the only exercise you can do here is flex the muscles over and over. Just don't strain too much. It may be too many miles to the next rester or fooder.

LEGS - The left leg is no problem here. It is usually just hanging around anyway. Put it flat on the floor and attempt to push down. If you can reach the firewall, push against that. The right leg presents a minor problem. Its time is pretty much taken up with the gooser, unless, of course, you have autopilot. As a matter of fact, about the only way to exercise the right leg is if your automobile is equipped with autopilot. If you do have autopilot, right leg exercises are similar to left leg exercises. If you do not have autopilot, about the only thing you can do is stop at a rester and stretch.

NECK - These exercises are simple and effective. You can tilt your head from side to side, twist left to right, and tilt forwards and backwards. This last movement is sort of like slow motion whiplash. Just make sure to lower the headrest first. Remember that when performing neck exercises, your eyes will be off the road for short periods of time. Make sure you are maintaining sufficient dash coefficient to be able to react if necessary. Nothing like putting your eyes back on the road only to see the coroader in front of you has stopped. And if you wear bifocals, there will be that refocusing time.

BUTTOCKS - Flex exercises work here. That ol' Gluteus Maximus takes the brunt of all the driveage you put it through. Twist your hips from side to side and shift from cheek to cheek. Again, this is one of those areas which is hard to exercise while your vehicle is in motion.

So the real solution seems to be to pull into the next rester or fooder and get out of the automobile. Nothing like a walk around the rester or fooder to keep the juices flowing. One form of exercise which can be performed while on such an excursion is called Sneaker Squeaking and can be particularly irritating to anyone else nearby. Sneaker Squeaking is simply the act of rubbing your sneaker-clad feet on the floor of the fooder in such a way as to make as much noise as possible. This is a form of exercise because of the muscle movements involved in twisting and turning the legs and ankles. Of course, if you have on loafers, you will not irritate anyone, but you will not know if you are getting the proper amount of exercise.

If you do decide to leave the comfortable confines of your automobile and it is raining, make other plans. Run like a madman or madwoman through the raindrops.

I, 95
_____

QUESTION: How many bones are there in the human hand?

GLOSSARY

ACCIDENTDOM
The state of being in an accident.

AR
Alternate Route. Use ARs when 1) flashing 1610 signs indicate that there is a backup on the I, or 2) you need a break from the I.

AU
Audio Unit. The radio/tape/CD player in the crashboard of your car.

AUNTIE EMM
An Automatic Teller Machine. These are appearing more and more in fooders, and they are guaranteed to not accept the card you are carrying. If you can't pay the duty, find an AR.

AUTOPILOT
Cruise control.

AUTORAG
Any soft material (preferably cotton), previous-life garment with one small hole or scar which renders it no longer wearable. This qualifies it as material to clean the automobile.

AUTOTATOR
The driver of a vehicle. See CO-AUTOTATION.

I, 95

AUTOTUDE
The demeanor one assumes while on the I.

BAGGY
The white inflatable unit which keeps your noggin from meeting the windshield or steerage unit at high rates of speed. Also known as the Air Bag, Supplemental Restraint System, SRS.

BEAMERS
A roader who insists on keeping their high beams on all the time, usually blinding someone. Beamers suffer from Blueblindness.

BEDROOM
Mobile home. Also referred to as "Winnies," short for Winnebago.

BINDERS
those units which are used to slow down and/or stop the vehicle, commonly referred to as brakes.

BLOCK
The group of cars in front of you driving side by side taking up all the available lanes and doing the speed limit. Hopefully not UMCs.

BLOWING
Depressing the inner ring of the Steerage Unit. On newer automobiles, depressing the button symbolized with a cornet. Also known as horn-honking or beeping.

BLOWUP
An inflatable dummy used to attempt to make dummies out of State Troopers. Not a good move.

BLUE
Actually called *The* Blue, this is the windshield washer fluid you never have when your windshield is covered with dirt and/or bugs.

BLUEBLINDNESS
The inability of some autotators to discern the blue light in the cluster.

BLUESHOOTING
Spraying the autotator behind you with the Blue when they are following too closely, i.e., tailgating. Not to be confused with I-WASH.

BRAKE DANCE
The act of applying and unapplying just enough pressure to the brake pedal (BINDER) to allow the brake lights (REDS) to go on and off. Usually performed by Leffoots.

BUBBLES
Police Vehicles. Bubble Gum Machines (Outdated). See MC and UMC.

BUBBLESTOP
A traffic situation where a state trooper or other law enforcement official has pulled a vehicle over to the side of the road for a traffic violation. Usually results in rubbernecking, reds and a near jam condition.

I, 95

BUTT
Any contact with the rear portion of the automobile in front of you, or your rear portion with the front portion of the automobile behind you.

BUZZING
Lane changing to advance your position.

CIRCUS MAXIMUS
An I with five or more lanes of travel. Good for buzzing, but usually crowded. It is five or more lanes for good reason.

CLUSTER
The instrument panel containing Triple I which the average autotator usually ignores.

CO-AUTOTATION
Having someone (human coautotator) in the car with you while you drive. At a minimum, a copilot.

COROADER
Any other autotator on the same road with you. These people are great listeners will never give you any advise that you have to heed, or even listen to. Better than a copilot.

COW
A Leather Throne; any item covered with leather.

CRASHBOARD
The area directly beneath the windshield where, in an accident without a baggy, you will park your face if not belted.

DARKSIDE
I driveage (or any other function) performed after the sun sets.

DASH
The white line in the middle of the I. The typical dash is ten feet long and separated from the next dash by thirty feet, making the dash-to-dash frequency forty feet. Seems like a lot less at 70 miles-per-hour.

DIQ
Driving Intelligence Quotient. An amount of smarts which enables an autotator to attain Point B-ing. The bigger the DIQ, the easier to attain Point B-ing.

DOT
Department Of Transportation. The initial of the state is usually inserted in front, i.e., Virginia is VDOT, making it impossible to tell apart from the Vermont Department of Transportation.

DRAIN AND FILL
The act of stopping at a fooder or rester, Sloaning, and buying another cup of coffee or soda.

DREAMILE
The distance traveled while the autotator was daydreaming. Usually nothing of the dreamile is remembered.

I, 95

DRIVEAGE
The act of driving and the luminous radiance which should be maintained while driving.

DUNCH
See any good dictionary.

DUTY BOOTH
A means whereby a state collects coin of the realm for a Federal Highway which your taxes have already paid for.

ELEPHANT TRACKS
Large dashes or painted areas indicating an exit ramp. (See SKIP LINES and PUPPY FEET.)

FOLDAGE
The act of folding a road map to its original configuration after it has been opened to it's fullest and refolded so as to display the section of the I you are currently traversing[113].

FOODER
A rester with food.

GO RED
Apply the brakes.

---

[113] Known throughout the Mercator world as "Reverse Lateral Contractive Mappage," to be covered in a later book.

GOOSER
The pedal on the floor of most vehicles which, when depressed, supplies fuel to the carburetor/fuel injectors, thus motivating the vehicle in the direction indicated by the PRNDL.

I
Interstate. Where this all takes place. Where you would rather not be, especially when it would be so nice to be someplace else, which is why you are on the I.

I-WASH
Cleaning your windshield when in a lane of vehicles traveling at or above the speed limit. Not to be confused with BLUESHOOTING.

JAM
A quantity of automobiles whose common karma is to be stopped on a road to observe the Ambulance Dance that someone else initiated. (See NEAR JAM.)

JUPITER EFFECT
A condition which cannot be predicted or defined. Similar to "everything else", but different. So named because there is no car named The "Jupiter," unless, of course, GM has started another division.

LCU
Liquid Containment Unit. A container for the liquid which you intend to imbibe to keep you awake while driving. Should be insulated.

I, 95

LEFFOOT
A person who drives with their left foot on the brake pedal, thus keeping the brake light on while doing 70 miles per hour, and confusing the devil out of everyone when they do actually apply the brakes.

LEFTY
A person who insists that driving in the left hand (passing) lane is the only way to travel. Usually not the fastest autotator on the I at the time.

LEO
Law Enforcement Officer.

LTT
Liquid Transfer Task. A difficult but necessary task performed while driving.

MAPPAGE
The ability to read and interpret road maps. A requirement for AR creation. Does NOT include the ability to fold a map once it has been unfolded. (See FOLDAGE.)

MC
Marked Car, usually with "bubble gum machines" and loud piercing whistles. Alternatively, Bubbles. See UMC.

MIDDLE MUSHROOM
A roader doing the speed limit or less in the middle of a trilane.

MOM 'N' POP
A Rental Van (driven by Pop) and a station wagon or sedan (driven by Mom because she doesn't want to or shouldn't be driving the van) traveling at or below the speed limit in the right lane (thank you thank you thank you) moving to greener pastures. The kids took a plane because they get car or van sick.

MUSHROOM
A slow LEFTY.

NEAR JAM
A state of driveage where there is a high density of automobiles, but all vehicles are maintaining the speed limit. One slip by any coroader will in all probability result in a Jam. (See JAM.)

OFFICIALS
Bubble occupants.

PACK
A group of coroaders so insecure that they insist on traveling the I together as close together as possible. Similar to a BLOCK, but not necessarily blocking traffic. Usually members of SIN (Safety In Numbers.)

PATELLAGE
Manipulating the steerage unit with one's knee or knees while both hands are employed in other activities, usually the LTT. See PINKAGE.

I, 95

PEDIDDLE
Also "Pididdle", any vehicle with one headlight extinguished. A less used variation is Elddidep, which, of course, is a vehicle with one taillight out. A vehicle with both headlights or taillights out is called a "Redneck Porch Swing."

PEDS
Roaders without vehicles. Commonly referred to as pedestrians and destined to get in your way at some point in your travels, but not usually on the I, except in resters and fooders.

PINKAGE
Steering with the pinkie finger only. To be performed at incredibly slow or incredibly fast speeds only. Sometimes performed during LTT. (See Patellage.)

POINT B-ING
The act of getting carefully and safely from Point A to Point B. A state of Mind.

POKER
A Pokin' Roader.

POKIN'
Driving slowly, anywhere, but primarily in the rightmost lane, where it is perfectly legal.

PORTASIGNAGE
Portable signage used by DOTs to indicate temporary traffic situations.

PRNDL
Pronounced "Prndl" (and always capitalized), the indicator on the steerage column or floor next to the "stick" which indicates the relative direction you desire the vehicle to travel. Not found in vehicles requiring motivation with the left foot.

PSYCHOAUTOLYZE
To analyze the driveage habits (AUTOTUDE) of the coroaders within two-tenths of a mile of your vehicle.

PUPPY FEET
Small dashes leading to an exit ramp. (See also SKIP LINES and ELEPHANT TRACKS.)

PURE RED
The locking up of the tires by standing on the brake pedal. On automobiles equipped with Anti-Lock Braking systems, there is no good indication that the vehicle in front has just gone pure red. Usually the tires smoke.

QUADLANE
An I with four lanes of travel.

QUARTER UP
Looking ahead ¼ mile to assess traffic situations or discern appropriate signage.

REDS
A traffic situation where a majority of the coroaders have their brake lights on, for whatever reason.

I, 95

REPACK
To join up with another group of coroaders after stopping at a fooder or rester. Requires autotude readjustment.

RESTER
A rest area without a restaurant, but possibly with venders. At a minimum there are rooms in which to rest.

RIRMIR
The looking glass situated at the top inside of the front window or the outside door. The rirmir on the outside of the right door (if equipped) is from the arcade gallery and will make you look very funny if you put your nose up close to it.

ROADER
You and all the other autotators out there on the I. Anyone on the road.

ROYAL SLOAN
The Loo, John, Toilet, Crapper, Urinal. Also known as American Standard.

ROY'S
Also, THE ROY'S. A generic term for fooders, so established because of the quantity of Roy Rogers restaurants on the I.

RPM
Raised (or Recessed) Pavement Marker. The relatively new way to mark lanes. These are reflectors which are embedded in the pavement and rise $3/16^{ths}$ of an inch to help mark lanes, increasing visibility after dark or when there is rain on the pavement and the skip lines are not entirely clear.

RUBBER
This is not a book on Sex Education or the Prevention of Diseases. This is simply your tires and the material of which they are made.

SKIP LINES
Dashes. (See also PUPPY FEET and ELEPHANT TRACKS.)

SLOAN (verb)
Use the "facilities," especially necessary after consuming much too much coffee.

SLOWAGE
Pulling into one of the middling lanes and reducing speed.

STEERAGE, IN
Grasping the Steerage Unit so as to direct the automobile in such a way as to achieve Point B-ing.

STEERAGE UNIT
The steering wheel. The unit that points the rubber in the direction you determine. On newer models, this contains the baggy.

TAKER
The ever-so-pleasant human being who always has their hand out for you to fill with Coin of the Realm. Takers can be found in fooders and duty booths.

TC
Trash Can.

TE
Traffic Equilibrium. The state of driveage in which all autotators drive perfectly and maintain proper speeds and distances from each other and are happy doing it. An impossible state.

THRONE
Your driving chair. The seat in front of the steerage.

TRILANE
The three lane I. The most common.

TRIPLE I
Incredibly Important Information is driveage information which transcends the mundane. Includes a multitude of various data, from your lane going red to signage such as "Continuous Pachyderm Crossing."

UMC
UnMarked Car. Virginia has UM Vans.

VENDER
A vending machine in a rest area. Usually non-functional. The coinage required to operate a vender is outrageous so Auntie Emm is usually there, but not usually willing to take your card.

QUIZ ANSWERS

PROLOGUE:

A *gloss* is a brief explanatory note. A *glossary* is a collection of glosses.

INTRODUCTION:

4,092. There are 175,128,000 (1994 numbers) licensed drivers[114] and 42,795 miles of I.

SPACE:

175° to 180° Fahrenheit.

DRIVEAGE:

Eighteen gallons.

---

[114] There are 89 million men and 86 million women. The difference is the number of male NASCAR drivers versus the number of female NASCAR drivers.

I, 95

I GAMES:

53. All 50 state plates plus the District of Columbia, the U.S. Virgin Islands, and Diplomat plates. Of course, it could be argued that there are an additional nine plates from Canada, but, hey, this is America!

JAMS:

Young drivers learn to drive on driveways. Old drivers join jams and park on parkways.

I POLICE:

A surprisingly low 20,000 miles. Sources at the Maryland State Police vehicle hospital tell me that some of their vehicles are 10 years old and DO have 200,000 miles on them.

SIGNAGE:

Red signage indicates that you are in a potentially dangerous situation. "Wrong Way" signs are red. If you are facing one of these, you have performed some incredibly asinine maneuver.

ETIQUETTE:

The fork is in the middle of the road.

DUTY BOOTHS:

A typical day sees 128,788 vehicles pass through[115]. That's 89.5 vehicles per minute, all day long.

TRUCKIN':

First of all, there is no such thing as an "average" semi, since they are one of the most customizable vehicles on the road. They can have up to 18 forward gears. Most have somewhere between 9 and 15.

LANEAGE:

Many different things. Some dashes are made of tape. Some are made of thermoplastics or epoxies applied like paint, but environmental considerations have pretty much negated the use of these. The most common is a water-based paint called waterborn. Included in the paint are glass beads about half the size of a pencil lead which will reflect your headlights.

I NICETIES:

According to one WA (Washroom Attendant), the Men's Room goes through "not very much,[116]" and the Ladies Room goes through two cases, or about 24 rolls.

---

[115] Thanks to the very helpful people at the Travel Center at the Maryland House. This figure is Southbound only and was collected on Monday, February 12, 1995.

I, 95

FOODAGE:

1. Bullet
2. Savannah, Georgia

PLACE NAMES:

Yes. Between 11 P.M. and 3:30 A.M.

MAPPAGE:

Thomas Jefferson set up the first United States Public Land Survey system which was to map the entire known United States.

ODDITIES:

Rumblestrip Skin.

---

[116] "Much" is defined as "a great quantity;" "Very Much" is defined as "a very great quantity;" "Not very much" is defined as "not a very great quantity." All this translates to "Some."

1610 AM:

Guglielmo Marconi (1874 - 1937) sent the first transatlantic wireless transmission from Poldhu, Cornwall to St. John's, Newfoundland in 1911.

CONSTRUCTION:

There are approximately 42,795 miles of I in the United States. The cost to construct this mileage was approximately 124.9 billion dollars. That comes out to $2,918,565.26 per mile[117].

EXERCISE:

There are 8 Carpal bones, 5 Metacarpal bones and 14 phalanges, for a total of 27 bones.

---

[117] Grolier's Encyclopedia.

I, 95

Many, many thanks to ....

My proofreader and daughter Jennifer

Bob Stall for his help and his patience with my prodding

My worst critic and best sister Lisa

My best friend and worst critic Lanny

The coroaders of New Jersey who put up with me while they also had to put up with each other.

Dave Wildroudt at the Maryland Transportation Authority for the wildly enthusiastic responses to my seemingly stupid questions.

The Very Short State of Delaware[118]

All the state highway maintenance crews without whom my trips would have been intolerably shorter.

Judy at VDOT

Lisa, Butch, Dave, Bryan, Tom, Tommy, and the rest of the crew at Bennigans for the space, the time, and the wings.

All the Takers I have had the pleasure of dealing with.

William Visser at the Wayne, New Jersey AAA

David for watching the girls for me while I was away

---

[118] 15.5 miles from Top-Dead-Center Delaware Memorial Bridge to the Maryland state line.

I, 95

This page is not blank…..

I, 95

About the Arthur...

Born in Newfoundland, Canada in 1948, AB feels like he has been driving since then. His father taught him how to autotate at an early age on an island off of the coast of Maine. His father thought this island training would be much safer for everyone. AB's father believed that any vacation with the children should include a tortuous, un-air-conditioned voyage on an I which lasted at least 45% of the vacation time allotted. These vacations included I voyages from Washington, D.C. to the same island off of the coast of Maine, even before there was an entire I through Baltimore. Needless to say, there were many times when AB's father would rather have let the children out on the side of the road.

AB lives in Virginia with his incredibly understanding wife, stepson, and two wonderful daughters, all of whom are licensed drivers.